Stakeholder Relationship Management

Stakeholder Relationship Management

A Maturity Model for Organisational Implementation

LYNDA BOURNE

GOWER

Published by
Gower Publishing Limited
Wey Court East
Union Road
Farnham
Surrey, GU9 7PT
England

Ashgate Publishing Company
Suite 420
101 Cherry Street
Burlington,
VT 05401-4405
USA

www.gowerpublishing.com

British Library Cataloguing in Publication Data
Bourne, Lynda.
 Stakeholder relationship management : a maturity model for
 organisational implementation.
 1. Social responsibility of business. 2. Reengineering
 (Management)
 I. Title
 658.4'08-dc22

 ISBN: 978-0-566-08864-3 (hbk)
      978-0-566-09193-3 (ebk)

Library of Congress Cataloging-in-Publication Data
Bourne, Lynda.
 Stakeholder relationship management : a maturity model for organisational
implementation / by Lynda Bourne.
    p. cm.
 Includes bibliographical references and index.
 ISBN 978-0-566-08864-3 (hardback) -- ISBN 978-0-566-09193-3 (ebook)
 1. Corporate governance. 2. Industrial management. I. Title.
 HD2741.B68 2009
 658--dc22

                                                              2009018881

Mixed Sources
Product group from well-managed forests and other controlled sources
www.fsc.org Cert no. SA-COC-1565
© 1996 Forest Stewardship Council
FSC

Printed and bound in Great Britain by
MPG Books Ltd, Bodmin, Cornwall.

Contents

List of Figures

List of Tables

Acknowledgements

I have probably written millions of words about stakeholder relationship management, and now the ideas have all come together in one book. I'm told that the first book is the hardest. And it has been a difficult journey, but worthwhile. To those people who helped in this journey I am deeply grateful.

To Patrick, my long-suffering spouse, thank you for your support, ideas, debates and practical assistance.

To Jo Stephenson, my colleague and friend, thank you for the countless hours you spent reading all the chapters and helping me find the right tone for this book.

To Jonathan Norman at Gower Publishing, thank you for your assistance in this journey.

To my countless colleagues, students, clients and friends who have contributed to these ideas from their experience, you helped me turn a doctoral research paper into a useful, usable set of guidelines to further the cause of stakeholder relationship management in organisations around the world.

Thank you.

Foreword

At the time of writing this, the world is going through the worst financial and economic crisis in recent history. Few – if any – had predicted the crisis when APM Terminals back in 2007 launched its journey towards a stronger stakeholder engagement culture. Looking back I am glad we did! In an infrastructure industry like the ports industry good, genuine stakeholder relations are fundamental to business success – with suppliers, customers, authorities, partners, NGOs and so on. Those relationships are even more important in a time of crisis.

When we launched the stakeholder engagement programme within our Business Development and Investment Unit our focus was on developing and implementing a practical and down to earth approach which delivers tangible improvements to our business results. Our main business driver was to increase our success in winning new tenders and landing new deals for developing port infrastructure, as well as successfully managing stakeholders during the actual development and construction of the ports. Although it had always been clear to us that stakeholder relations were key to our success we had never taken a focused approach to improving our capabilities and focus in this area.

Early on we recognised that there was good practical help to be found externally and engaged Lynda Bourne to support us in developing our tool kit and implementation approach. One of the main reasons for choosing to work with Lynda was the clarity and intuitive logic of the *Stakeholder* Circle methodology, but also the fact that the methodology and approach could easily be adjusted to our level of maturity and ambition. We were from the outset determined that Stakeholder Engagement should not be overcomplicated and were humble about our starting point.

In addition to the application of the *Stakeholder* Circle as a tool, we had an ambition to also make this a cultural journey towards becoming more externally focused and more focused on developing lasting stakeholder relationships. To achieve this we decided to roll out our stakeholder engagement approach through a number of workshops making it a key pillar in what we call our 'Winning Approach'. It is now well embedded into our organisation and all new investment opportunities we look at will go through a stakeholder analysis – with consequent actions.

Following the roll-out within our Business Development and Investment Unit several other parts of our organisation have adopted our approach in part or fully.

For me personally it has been a great learning process, where working with the **Stakeholder** *Circle* methodology and seeing it applied in practice has made stakeholder engagement an intuitive part of what I focus on as a leader.

For project managers and business people in general I recommend reading *Stakeholder Relationship Management: A Maturity Model for Organisational Implementation*: be inspired to make structured stakeholder engagement a natural part of your focus.

Klaus Rud Sejling
Vice President, Head of Global Business Development,
APM Terminals,
The Hague, Netherlands

Preface

To summarise: it is a well-known fact that those people who most want to rule people are, ipso facto, those least suited to do it. To summarise the summary: anyone who is capable of getting themselves made President should on no account be allowed to do the job. To summarise the summary of the summary: people are a problem.

Douglas Adams – The Restaurant at the End of the Universe

Unless you are a hermit living alone in a cave ten days' journey from the nearest settlement and without any means of communication with the outside world, you will need to deal with people! In the everyday 'stuff' that we do, both personal and business, we will need to work with, or build connections with, people. These connections, relationships, may vary in their timespan, in their strength and in their purpose. We can't ignore these relationships. Often we can't even choose which ones we will need to invest our time and attention in. As my grandmother used to say: 'We can choose our friends but not our family.' We often can't choose our work relationships either.

The other important consideration about relationships is that we need to constantly work on developing and maintaining them, whether they are personal or business-related. Relationships with friends and family need constant reinforcement, and so do business relationships. They require constant maintenance in the form of appropriate communication, and the communication must be tied to the needs and requirements of that relationship, for example, flowers and dinner for a spouse's birthday or appropriate targeted information for an important organisational stakeholder. We usually know where we need to focus our personal relationship management activities, but it is not so easy to know where we must build business relationships, whether short-term or long-term. There are numerous sources of advice and instructions for building and maintaining personal relationships, but much less has been written about building and maintaining relationships in the business world. This book seeks to address that deficiency, firstly by discussing why stakeholders matter, secondly through the description of a structured, flexible approach that provides a basis for monitoring and measuring the effectiveness of the communication – the **Stakeholder** *Circle®* – and finally through developing a set of guidelines for organisations that seek to implement this methodology, or any other, for improved stakeholder relationship management.

Processes and practices leading to communication planning and basic stakeholder analysis have been a part of organisations' management toolkits and methodologies for many years. However, until recently, stakeholder relationship management seems to have been a secondary consideration, part of the 'soft skills' element of managing the progress of an organisation's activity: written and spoken about but rarely taken seriously. There seems to be a fixed view enshrined in practice that stakeholder analysis only needs to be done once, that there must be a limit to the stakeholder community, and a guess about the stakeholder's ability to impact the work is sufficient. The people side of an organisation's work is seen to be secondary to managing budgets, schedules, scope and risk. In the work I have done in organisations in Australia, Europe and the US, data maintained in the activity's risk management documentation has shown that risks about people (stakeholders) will usually make up over 90% of the risk management plan. However, even this connection between risk management and stakeholder management comes as a surprise to most of the managers I have discussed this connection with.

In my own work in the corporate world both as a project manager and as a senior manager, often a sponsor of projects, I formed the view that people were always the 'problem' when projects or other organisational activities encountered problems or failed to deliver to requirements. People were at the centre of the issue whether it was a breakdown in communication flows, support or resources withheld, or a failure to deliver on commitments. I started to see these issues as failures of relationships between the activity or project and its people (stakeholders) and realised that more needed to be done in two specific areas. Firstly, a more structured approach to developing targeted communication to the 'right' stakeholders. The second approach to provide more assistance to organisations in implementing new or improved processes and practices for stakeholder relationship management.

When the relationships between the activity and its stakeholders failed, the activity was deemed to have failed by some or all of its stakeholders. The perception of 'failure', or of not delivering, is unique to each individual or group with a stake in the activity. If there is a belief that some aspect of a stakeholder's requirements or expectations has not been adequately met, then there will be the perception that the activity has failed.

How does the team manage the perceptions of their stakeholders? It is a matter of considered analysis of all those groups and individuals to understand their needs and build relationships. The development and improvement of the *Stakeholder* Circle methodology occurred over many years through academic research, publication in academic journals, presentations at conferences and modifications and improvements through working with organisations and practitioners in implementing stakeholder relationship management.

Just as people do, organisations operate at different levels of efficiency and readiness for change. In the area of stakeholder relationship management organisations will exhibit different levels of readiness to embrace the use of stakeholder relationship management processes and practices. At one level of maturity the development of sophisticated mapping techniques that can be used for predictive reporting, reviews and health checks will assist an organisation in improving its competitive advantage. At lower levels of maturity organisations may gradually develop consistent processes and practices that support structured understanding of the stakeholder community.

My intention in writing this book was to provide in one place a comprehensive account of stakeholder relationship management. By providing practitioners, organisational executives and researchers with information to assist them, I hope to be able to raise the profile of stakeholder relationship management in all areas. I anticipate that this book will meet the needs of organisations at all levels of maturity. It is intended to provide information to assist organisations in taking their own next step towards improving knowledge and willingness to build and maintain robust relationships with those who matter to the success of their activities.

A CD is included with this book to help readers start on the journey of improving stakeholder relationship management. It contains:

- a 30-day trial version of the *Stakeholder* Circle database (SIMS). Chapter 4 provides more details, and a help function is included in the software;

- a self-running PowerPoint presentation of the features of all the software tools that support the *Stakeholder* Circle;

- the *stakeholder-on-a-page* template, for small teams or organisations beginning the journey of stakeholder relationship management;[1]

- a Quick Reference Guide to assist in running workshops. It contains a summary of all the statements that assist the team in analysing the stakeholder community;

- a number of conference papers and journal articles describing applications of the processes and practices supported by the **Stakeholder** *Circle* methodology. These papers are listed below.

The Paradox of Project Control This paper explores the hypothesis that, within complex matrix organisations, the 'zone' between the strategic vision set by senior management and the projects created to fulfil it, is a highly complex and dynamic organism. Stimulus to the organism may, or may not produce change. The change may be slight or catastrophic, beneficial or detrimental, and cannot be predicted. Succeeding in this environment needs a different management paradigm from that developed for management in traditional project industries. Stakeholder relationship management is central to managing within this environment.

Visualising Stakeholder Influence, Two Australian Examples Using a case study and action learning approach, this paper draws upon emerging project management and wider strands of management decision-making literature. The results of the analysis described in the paper showed significant differences in the processes needed to manage the different stakeholder groups. Project teams involved in the research recognised that they needed to adopt significantly different strategies to achieve stakeholder engagement, leading to stakeholder satisfaction and a successful project. The **Stakeholder** *Circle* database tool (SIMS) was found by the case study respondents to be useful and that it also complemented and enhanced risk management approaches.

Developing Stakeholder Engagement Maturity in APM Terminals Management BV: An International Case Study Engaging effectively and ethically with key stakeholders to help create a successful project outcome requires significant levels of skill and organisational maturity. This paper defines a five-level model of Stakeholder Relationship Management Maturity (SRMM®) and provides a means for organisations to identify their own level of 'readiness' for

---

1   The use of this tool as well as the SIMS database and the SWS spreadsheet is described in Chapter 4.

the introduction of stakeholder engagement practices and to identify areas of potential improvement.

From Commander to Sponsor: Managing Upwards in a Project Environment   This paper focuses on the critical project management survival skill of engaging senior managers, and of 'helping them help you'. Data from case studies will define the framework of the 'command and control' school of traditional management practice, providing the foundation for discussion of the techniques that will assist moving management thinking towards the 'sponsor' school. The techniques include establishing a reputation for trustworthiness and effective delivery of results, managing the expectations, and therefore the support, of key senior stakeholders using influence networks, targeted communication and plain persistence, based on the *Stakeholder* Circle methodology and toolset.

Practice Note: Advancing Theory and Practice for Advancing Stakeholder Management in Organisations   The aim of this paper is to report on the advancement, in theory and practice, in stakeholder management as a result of the author's experiences, and to invite other practitioners and researchers to collaborate in, or contribute to, research to further advance stakeholder management theory and practice in both project management and organisations. The Stakeholder Relationship Management Maturity approach to assisting organisations successfully implement a stakeholder 'mindset' or culture, has been developed to the level described in this paper through a process of reflection, action research and continuous improvement. This paper provides a framework that any individual or organisation can use as a basis for immediate implementation of stakeholder relationship management in any project or organisation.

Introducing a Stakeholder Management Methodology into the EU   This paper describes the introduction of the *Stakeholder* Circle methodology and software into the European Union by Tiba Managementberatung GmbH, the German partner of Stakeholder Management P/L. The focus of this paper is an analysis of the issues and challenges faced by Tiba to develop and refine an effective strategy for the introduction of the methodology into the diverse corporate and national cultures present in the EU market place. A key element will be an assessment of the overall EU project management community to determine if there is a common EU culture or if differences in both PM maturity, national and organisational culture make the concept of an *EU marketplace* for project management processes and tools a dangerous illusion.

Managing relationships both personal and business is something that everyone (except the hermit) needs to do: anyone reading this book should take away ideas and practices that will help them achieve this. Building relationships and maintaining the most effective level of engagement does not have to be impossible, and I hope this book helps. Good luck in your endeavours.

Dr Lynda Bourne, PMP, FAIM, CMACS
CEO, Stakeholder Management Pty Ltd,
Melbourne, Australia

SECTION I

Framework

Introduction

In early 2008, HM Queen Elizabeth opened British Airways' (BA) new terminal building, Heathrow Terminal 5 (T5), with glowing words. For at least twelve months before that T5 had become part of the mythology of the UK construction industry as a symbol of how the industry had turned itself around. The elements of this miraculous improvement were the introduction of innovative building and contracting practices that resulted in a record low accident rate measured in terms of lost time days and a delivery ahead of schedule and under budget. Yet when T5 was opened for commercial air traffic, chaos ensued! Passengers lost their bags, flights were delayed or cancelled, and T5 was no longer seen as a symbol of innovation, but as a stain on BA's reputation. The theme of T5 is the theme of this book: that the success of organisational change depends on:

- People and their:

    - perception of success or failure;

    - willingness to participate in the vision of the organisation as defined by management.

In the same way the failure of organisational change can be caused by:

- Poor integration of the different parts of the change, for example:

    - the build and develop phase goes well but implementation is poorly executed;

    - the infrastructure is based on complex technology that is totally inaccessible to those who must use it regularly.

- Failure of management to recognise that success criteria should be broader than bottom line considerations:

    - shareholder value is not the only business driver;

    - organisations are now expected to consider socially beneficial behaviours such as sustainability and corporate social responsibility as part of their mission and vision.

The story of Heathrow Terminal 5 will not be analysed in depth in this book, but some aspects of that project will be used to illustrate the point of the book. That point is that many organisations have followed the management ideologies of the bottom line above all else, shareholder value is paramount and the CEO should be a hero. The premise of this book is that for any activity an organisation undertakes, whether strategic, operational or tactical, the activity can only be successful with the input, commitment and support of people – stakeholders. Gaining and maintaining the support and commitment of stakeholders requires a continuous process of engaging the right stakeholders at the right time and understanding and managing their expectations.

The book is intended to provide managers with a framework for successful stakeholder relationship management. Success in managing stakeholder relationships is achieved through a long-term commitment to a structured process focused on:

- identifying stakeholders;

- understanding their expectations;

- managing those expectations;

- monitoring the effectiveness of stakeholder engagement activities;

- continuous review of the stakeholder community.

Creating a stakeholder-aware culture in an organisation requires a structured approach, skilful management and time. As a continuous improvement process, stakeholder management requires understanding and support, or awareness, from everyone in the organisation ranging from the CEO to the short-term contractor. This ensures the concepts and practices of effective stakeholder relationship management become embedded in the culture of the organisation: 'how we do things around here'.

This book will provide a structured approach to assist organisations achieve these objectives. There are two road maps: the first provides structured guidelines for organisations to identify current stakeholders, and the means to understand and manage the expectations of these stakeholders. This structure is provided by the *Stakeholder Circle*®[1] methodology for stakeholder engagement.

The second road map provides guidance for organisations wishing to implement this, or any other appropriate methodology in the most effective way. The Stakeholder Relationship Management Maturity (SRMM®)[2] model has been developed to assist the implementation of stakeholder management processes and practices that most meet the organisation's current level of readiness for stakeholder relationship management. By using the SRMM assessment guidelines the organisation can understand its starting point for improvement. SRMM also provides guidance on what processes and practices might be most effective at the current phase in the organisation's development. Using a structured assessment process places the organisation in the best position to measure and obtain evidence of the effectiveness of the improved processes and practices.

Many organisations are familiar with the concept of organisational maturity. The three best known are:

- Capability Maturity Model Integration (CMMI): developed by Carnegie Mellon's Software Engineering Institute (SEI) as a tool for assessment and improvement of an organisation's software development processes and practices.

- Organizational Project Management Maturity Model (OPM3): developed by the Project Management Institute (PMI) as a tool for assessment and improvement of an organisation's ability to choose the *right* projects and then do them *right* in a consistent manner.

- Portfolio, Programme and Project Management Maturity Model (P3M3): developed by the Office of Government Commerce (OGC) as a reference guide for structured best project and organisation practice.

---

1 *Stakeholder* Circle is a registered trademark of Mosaic Project Services Pty Ltd, Australia.
2 SRMM is a registered trademark of Practical PM Pty Ltd, Australia.

These three models are examples of a structured approach to organisational improvement that matches different stages of development with measurable goals. The CMMI approach is the basis for the concept of assessment, improvement and review that is the foundation of other maturity models. CMMI levels of maturity are defined as:

- initial;

- repeatable;

- defined;

- managed;

- optimising.

Since 2000, I have worked with organisations in Asia, Australasia, Europe and the US to develop ways for them to manage stakeholder relationships more effectively. These assignments involved training and consulting in stakeholder relationship management and the application of the stakeholder relationship management methodology developed as a result of this research. This methodology and supporting software tool, together called the *Stakeholder Circle,* have provided both individuals and organisations with practical insights and guidance in developing plans for managing relationships with stakeholders and monitoring the implementation and effectiveness of these plans.

This book will provide an organisation with resources for understanding and using processes and practices to identify and engage key stakeholders. It is organised in three sections:

- Section 1 is a theoretical framework providing the foundation for organisations to understand the importance of stakeholders to the work of the organisation and the nature of the stakeholder community and its membership.

- Section 2 is a guidebook on the most effective use of the *Stakeholder Circle* methodology to understand relationships that will exist between the activity and the stakeholder community and to develop and implement targeted communication.

- Section 3 describes SRMM and its application in assisting the most effective implementation of stakeholder relationship management in line with the culture of the organisation, its current business drivers and with the readiness of its people to embrace additional change. This section also offers a series of guidelines and milestones for achieving the preferred or most appropriate level of maturity in stakeholder relationship management.

The primary focus of all three sections is to support individuals and organisations in improving stakeholder management in endeavours as diverse as:

- organisational corporate social responsibility (CSR) obligations;

- competitor analysis;

- analysis of parties involved in bids;

- organisational change programmes;

- delivering successful marketing campaigns;

- projects, programs and portfolios;

- implementing new IT applications, including requirements definition, supply chain management;

- organisational support structures such as programme management offices (PMO);

- supporting organisational survival during major restructures, or mergers and acquisitions.

Table *i*.1 on the next page summarises the structure of the book.

Section I: Framework

Section I describes a framework for individuals and organisations to understand who the right stakeholders are at any point in time, and what these stakeholders require from success or failure of the organisation's work or its

Table *i*.1   Structure of the book

Section I: Framework	**Introduction** **Chapter 1: Why stakeholders matter** **Chapter 2: Who can be stakeholders?**
Section II: Guidebook	**Chapter 3: The right stakeholders** **Chapter 4: Mapping stakeholders** **Chapter 5: Measuring stakeholder *attitude*** **Chapter 6: Monitoring the engagement**
Section III: Implementation	**Chapter 7: Effective implementation** **Chapter 8: Defining organisational readiness** **Chapter 9: Implementation guidelines** **Chapter 10: Conclusion**

outcomes. Having identified the most important of these current stakeholders, the methodology supports the analysis, management and ongoing monitoring of relationships in this stakeholder community.

CHAPTER 1: WHY STAKEHOLDERS MATTER

Chapter 1 explores the idea of the importance of stakeholders to the success or failure of projects or other organisational endeavours through a study of a recent construction project – Heathrow's Terminal 5. It provides an argument for why stakeholders matter to the work that delivers the business strategy of an organisation. Through the analysis of this work and the outcomes of the work, it is possible to develop the following thesis: *success or failure depends on the views (perceptions) of stakeholders and also the passing of time.*

CHAPTER 2: WHO CAN BE STAKEHOLDERS?

Chapter 2 describes the emerging realisation of the importance of stakeholders to the success of an organisation, from a financial perspective but also from the perspective of their ability to influence an organisation's activities. It traces the development of the movement to include stakeholder engagement in the work of projects and programs and its gradual take-up in work beyond projects. The results of the analysis described in Chapters 1 and 2 lead to a description of the **Stakeholder** *Circle* – a five step methodology developed to assist project teams and then more recently, to assist organisations in managing stakeholder relationships.

Section II: Guidebook

CHAPTER 3: THE RIGHT STAKEHOLDERS

Chapter 3 describes the first two steps of the **Stakeholder** *Circle* methodology: *step 1: identify* and *step 2: prioritise*. The guidelines in this chapter enable the team to begin the stakeholder identification and prioritisation process. These processes also involve gathering essential data about each stakeholder to build appropriate and targeted communication.

CHAPTER 4: MAPPING STAKEHOLDERS

Chapter 4 describes various forms of stakeholder mapping before describing methods and templates within the methodology to reveal who has been identified as the most important stakeholders at this time. The mapping of *step 3: visualise* provides in one picture multiple dimensions of information about the stakeholder community.

CHAPTER 5: MEASURING STAKEHOLDER *ATTITUDE*

Chapter 5 describes *step 4: engage*, leading the team to analyse and document a view of the *attitude* of each of the community's important stakeholders and to identify where to focus most of its communication effort. Strategies and techniques for fine-tuning development and delivery of communication are also discussed.

CHAPTER 6: MONITORING THE ENGAGEMENT

Chapter 6 defines how to ensure the communication plans are implemented and how to measure the effectiveness of stakeholder communication – this is *step 5: monitor*.

Section III: Implementation

Section III describes Stakeholder Relationship Management Maturity (SRMM), a maturity model that helps an organisation identify its level of readiness to implement stakeholder management and engagement. Understanding its own level of readiness enables the organisation to target the appropriate elements for implementation of a stakeholder relationship management methodology. Too ambitious and the change effort is wasted; too little and the change is ignored: 'We are already doing this!'

CHAPTER 7: EFFECTIVE IMPLEMENTATION

Chapter 7 describes elements necessary for the successful implementation of the *Stakeholder* Circle in an organisation, and introduces the concept of maturity models and the SRMM.

CHAPTER 8: DEFINING ORGANISATIONAL READINESS

Chapter 8 describes the five SRMM levels, and the types of organisation that would correspond to these levels. An organisation should be able to identify its level of SRMM and from that identification plan and implement a programme to improve its stakeholder relationship management processes and practices.

CHAPTER 9: IMPLEMENTATION GUIDELINES

Chapter 9 describes practical guidelines for moving from one level of stakeholder relationship management maturity to another, supported by approaches based on the structure of the *Stakeholder* Circle methodology.

CHAPTER 10: CONCLUSION

Chapter 10 summarises the book and concludes with suggestions for further research.

1

Why Stakeholders Matter

Organisations, whether publicly listed (commercial), not-for-profit, or government bodies must deliver the strategies and requirements defined in their mission and vision, charter or articles of incorporation. The leadership team is accountable for the delivery of these strategies. Success is not necessarily or universally about delivering bottom line success. It can be defined in other ways depending on the corporate, legal, legislative or social responsibilities and requirements of the organisation. Success is bound up in how well the organisation conducts its activities, whether strategic, operational or tactical, to meet these requirements. Success is measured in part by reports of financial compliance, and in part by other less tangible aspects such as meeting expectations of its stakeholders (the public, government, shareholders, customers, employees, lobby groups or voters).

The organisation needs to focus on different sets of activities for the successful delivery of its vision, mission and business strategy. These activities fall into the following categories:

- Strategic: to deliver against the stated business plan for that reporting period. This may require:

    - development of new marketing, product or service strategies;

    - internal organisational change or improvement;

    - long-term response to changes in the business strategy because of changes to the industry;

    - responses to changes in the environment, whether business environment or natural environment;

    - new or adapted process and practices to meet new competitive threats or opportunities;

> – changes to adjust to changes in government policies.

- Operational: business as usual – whatever actions are needed to ensure effective and efficient delivery of the organisation's success criteria.

- Tactical or ad hoc: dealing with current issues or short term objectives. Sometimes this will be in the nature of a collection of projects or programs that together will deliver the organisation's strategy; sometimes this will take the form of dealing with unexpected issues or crises.

To perform any of these activities successfully or effectively, the organisation will need to put processes and practices in place to ensure:

- appropriate funding;

- measures of progress and success;

- assurances that resources can be made available when needed;

- standard processes to assist executive or leadership approval.

Organisations that 'do projects' will have many of these practices in place and will apply project management processes to all their activities. Other organisations may have other mechanisms in place to ensure the activities are accomplished and their agreed outcomes delivered.

Successful achievement of each activity will also inevitably require other organisations, groups or individuals to contribute to realisation of the agreed outcomes. These other organisations, groups or individuals, may be impacted upon by the work to accomplish the activity or by its outcomes. They are stakeholders whose needs, requirements and expectations must be considered as a necessary part of any organisation's planning and management. Successful organisations recognise that stakeholders contribute to the success or failure of their activities.

Research conducted on the success and failure of organisational activities has advanced many explanations for failure (or success) in the accomplishment of these activities. An analysis of this research and the responses of participants of workshops delivered on stakeholder relationship management since 2001[1] have shown no universal answer. However, the responses recognise the importance of other factors beyond the *iron triangle* of time, cost and scope, by identifying customers, senior managers, end users and often government as essential to organisation success.

This chapter defines the importance of stakeholders to the success or failure of the organisation's strategic objectives, operational activities or completion of tactical or ad hoc work. A study of a construction project completed in 2008 – Heathrow Terminal 5 – and its transition to an operational state serving British Airways' customers is used to demonstrate the ideas outlined. Through the analysis of this work and its outcomes, a proposal emerges suggesting that success, or failure, depends on the views (perceptions) of stakeholders, and that this perception may change over time. The first section summarises some recent research into success and failure of organisational activities, followed by a synthesis from this research to produce a view of organisation success or failure that is based on the effectiveness of managing relationships with key stakeholders through targeted communication. The final section describes the construction and operation of Heathrow T5 from the perspective of this synthesised view of success, concluding with a discussion of the implications for an organisation and its activities to deliver business strategy, meet operational requirements, or resolve tactical or ad hoc needs.

Research

When work to achieve organisational objectives fails, however these activities are managed or measured, the organisation is affected by its failure to achieve some part of its goals or requirements. As a consequence, scarce resources will be wasted and individuals and groups (stakeholders) who had expected some benefit from the successful accomplishment of the activity will be negatively impacted.

---

1 Workshops and courses conducted on stakeholder management from 2001 to 2009 with over 500 people include a discussion point on 'What is project success?' Responses always include 'within time, budget and scope', but generally also include reference to stakeholders in the form of 'customers are happy; stakeholders are satisfied; meets end-user needs'. Although such statements require additional clarification on 'How do you define happy?' or 'How do you know that they are satisfied?' it is an indication that those who attend this intermediate to advanced course have a level of sophistication that embraces the notion of the people side of project management.

The *triangle of dependence* (Sauer 1993) focused on the human aspects of IT project delivery and personal views of success. In this model project success or failure is strongly related to the perceptions of each individual stakeholder and his or her willingness and ability to act either for or against the work. This model has been adapted to the wider organisation by incorporating the work that any entity or group within the organisation may undertake to achieve the organisation's objectives. The adapted model is shown in Figure 1.1.

Any organisational activity has three components:

1.   processes and practices influenced by the organisation's culture that provide the framework, guidelines and measures to deliver the activity;

2.   supporters who provide funding, assistance or are beneficiaries;

3.   those who will actually plan, manage and execute the work.

As in the original model of the *triangle of dependence*, failure could be supporters' perceptions of expectations not met, or promises not delivered,

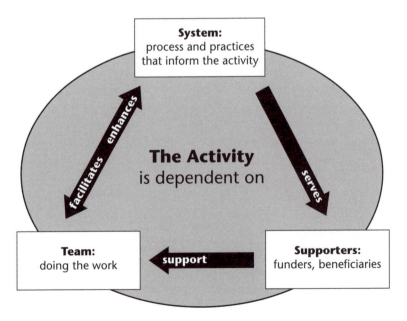

Figure 1.1   Adaptation of Sauer's *triangle of dependence*

or the belief that the support (resources) could be applied elsewhere. These perceptions are not necessarily based on logic, but often on the quality of the relationships between the project and its stakeholders. The organisation can expect to benefit from the innovations applied in delivering the activity, and from the new knowledge obtained and retained within the organisation. Whatever the benefit, it must be *perceived* to be so: the beneficiary must recognise that his or her expectations have been met.

Other research supports this model and defines failure as a combination of:

- poor alignment between the solution and the organisation's strategy, business requirements or priorities (KPMG 2005);

- lack of top management involvement and support (KPMG 2005);

- failure to acknowledge the behavioural aspects of risk (Murray-Webster and Hillson 2008);

- perception by stakeholders that the work has not delivered the expected outcomes or benefits (Sauer 1993; Lemon, Bowitz, Burn and Hackney 2002; Bourne and Walker 2003).

A SYNTHESIS OF THE RESEARCH

Integrating the results of this research provides a more holistic and balanced view (see Table 1.1 for a summary of this data). According to this approach, successful delivery of an organisation's activities requires attention to all of the following:

- alignment of the activity to the organisation's strategic, operational or tactical objectives (*delivery of value*);

- understanding and managing the expectations of stakeholders and fulfilling these managed expectations (*managing relationships*);

- appropriate, timely and consistent involvement by users and managers (*managing relationships*);

- timely (fearless) management of risk (*managing risk*).

Table 1.1   Success and failure categorised

Delivery of Value	Managing Risk	Managing Relationships
Appropriate and consistent use of management tools, processes and methodologies. *Requires commitment of team members, and encouragement of managers, to use tools, processes and methodologies.*	Identification and management of risk. *People account for a large proportion of risk:* • *Not delivering as committed;* • *Not supporting work and outcomes consistently;* • *Focus elsewhere (personal career, other work);* • *Not interested.*	Managing the expectations of stakeholders. *Research quoted above concludes that it is expectations not met, or perceptions of failure that will affect how stakeholders view the work or its outcomes. Stakeholders may not continue to support work that they perceive is not achieving to their expectations.*
Alignment of the outcomes of the activity to organisation strategy. *A governance body of senior management should be responsible for decisions on which work should be funded and resourced. The governance body also depends on advice regarding the work and whether it continues to deliver to the organisation's business requirements.*	Development of strategies for managing in environments of uncertainty. *Strategies will include regular progress reports on:* • *Tactical delivery of value (time, cost, scope)* • *Delivering business strategy* • *Procurement strategies to ensure sustainable mix of risk and cost sharing with suppliers, for long term relationships.*	Appropriate, timely and consistent involvement by users and managers. *Research has identified that a primary cause of failure is lack of appropriate involvement or removal of support by those who are impacted by, or can impact the work or its outcomes: the stakeholder.*
Appropriate skills and knowledge	Appropriate skills and knowledge	Appropriate skills and knowledge

In other words, successful management and delivery of an organisation's activities depends on balancing the conflicting requirements of:

• managing within the constraints of time, cost and quality;

• meeting the expectations of important stakeholders.

A Balanced View of Success

Figure 1.2 illustrates the interrelationships of the three elements:

1.   delivery of value;

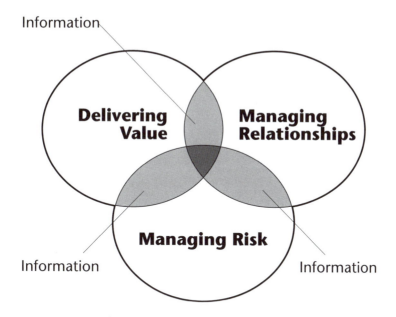

Figure 1.2   The interconnected elements of success

2.   management of risk;

3.   managing key relationships with stakeholders.

DELIVERY OF VALUE

The first of the three elements of success is the delivery of value to the organisation. Value, whether in the form of monetary or material worth, is delivered through both strategic and tactical means. Work to deliver specific or short term outcomes is usually of a tactical nature; aspects of strategic value are essential for long-term survival or success of the organisation.

Strategic value is described by:

- an organisation's governance strategies and practices;

- guidelines for the selection of work to deliver the organisation's strategic objectives as expressed in its business strategies;

- communication of these guidelines through publication of appropriate processes and measures;

- communication of the way the governance strategies and practices will be or are being implemented.

Tactical value describes activities such as:

- resolution of issues;

- delivering business strategy through projects or programs;

- communication through accurate, timely and focused reporting against delivery of tactical value.

COMMUNICATION RELATED TO VALUE

Delivering value, whether strategic or tactical, requires robust processes and practices to manage relationships with stakeholders through targeted communication in the form of regular reports, meetings, and presentations. Value is also delivered through managing risks by ensuring that the expectations of all stakeholders are met with regard to *what* is delivered as well as *when* and *how*. All of the messages used in the communication, whether standard reports or other types of information, must be focused on the needs of the stakeholders for specific information and not on the messages or information that the team thinks the stakeholder needs.

MANAGEMENT OF RISK

The second element is the management of risk (and exploitation of opportunity), within limits acceptable to the performing organisation. Risk management is about minimising potential risks while maximising potential opportunities.

Management of risk and opportunity can be considered both from a tactical and a strategic framework. Governance decisions manage strategic risk through:

- balancing delivery of business strategies;

- balancing tactical work and operational work;

- tracking the achievement of benefits to the organisation.

Managing risk focuses on using management disciplines to contend with uncertainty. Tactical aspects of risk include the risk analysis and management practices of the organisation.

PROCUREMENT AND RISK MANAGEMENT

The purpose of procurement management is to reduce the risk of acquiring outside goods and services. Procurement and contracts define risk sharing arrangements between buyers and suppliers in the organisational framework. An organisation must make decisions about whether to procure, how to procure, what to procure, how much to procure and when to procure. The negotiations that are part of contract preparation influence the nature of the relationships between the organisation and its suppliers: the better the relationship the more certain the successful completion of the activity or delivery of its outcomes. Procurement can be strategic through the development of partnerships and alliances with other organisations, and tactical through the development of contracts between specific activities and suppliers.

RISK BEHAVIOUR

The processes developed in risk management methodologies are built on an expectation that people will perform the planning, execution and monitoring of risk as defined in these methodologies. However, it is the behaviours around management of risk that are important for the success of risk management. Effective management of risk therefore requires recognising that people must implement the risk plans or act according to the plan if the risk event does occur, and putting in place mechanisms to monitor implementation and effectiveness of the risk responses.

COMMUNICATION RELATED TO RISK

Managing risk and the relationships necessary to reduce risk or to respond to risk events requires communication:

- Information about meeting the time, cost and scope of activities is essential to the management of risk.

- Risk plans communicate information about identified and prioritised risks to management.

- Risk plans communicate information about planned actions to individuals responsible for those actions.

- Contracts provide information about how the risk is shared between the activity and suppliers of goods and services (also stakeholders).

- The nature of the risk sharing arrangements influences the working relationships between the activity and the suppliers.

MANAGEMENT OF RELATIONSHIPS

The third element – managing relationships within and around the activity – includes balancing conflicting stakeholder needs and expectations. Legitimate and valid stakeholders need to be identified and their power and influence understood to manage their potential impact on an organisation's work or the outcomes of the work. Appropriate strategies can then be formulated and performed to maximise a stakeholder's positive influence and minimise any negative influence. This becomes a key risk-management issue for the team.

Each stakeholder's significance depends on the situation and the issues. The team cannot assume a supportive stakeholder on the first issue will be supportive on a second issue, or that a supportive stakeholder will continue to be supportive on that issue. Support must be sustained or obtained through communication, the only tool or technique available to manage relationships.

INTERDEPENDENCIES BETWEEN EACH OF THESE ELEMENTS

As is illustrated in Figure 1.2, each of the three elements overlaps the others, and all intersect. Stakeholders are central to success and failure in different ways, but the consistent theme is that *people are key*.

In summary, the key to successfully managing the people side of any endeavour is through communication, to report on the delivery of value and also to manage risk. Delivery of value is measured and communicated through the reporting mechanisms put in place by the organisation. These will be in the form of progress reports providing information to stakeholders about the actual progress of the work, highlighting issues or exceptions to focus management's attention. This information may also be useful to secure commitment of important stakeholders through imparting a feeling of confidence that the work is being properly managed. The reporting activity also contributes to managing risk through assuring important stakeholders that the work is in good hands and elevates the reputation and credibility of the activity's manager and team.

Successful delivery of an organisation's activities depends on an understanding that delivering successful outcomes to an organisation requires management of all three factors simultaneously. To try to isolate one element and focus only on that one, neglecting the others, is to miss the point of a balance of management actions.

The most important outcome of this analysis is to recognise that people are key in all of these elements, both from a tactical and a strategic perspective. Effective management of relationships requires planning and implementing communication that focuses on the groups or individuals that are important at each phase in the lifecycle of the work and understanding their requirements from the outcomes of the work. This will be described in more detail in later chapters.

Can an organisational activity deliver its outcome *on time, on budget* and still be considered a failure, despite delivering 100 per cent of its scope? The answer must be 'Yes, it can, because people are the key to success or failure!' Other factors can influence the perception (and possible reality) of how successful an activity may be. The process of building Heathrow's Terminal 5 and its public opening in 2008 is a good example of how different stakeholders will have conflicting perception of success (or failure) depending on their experiences and expectations, and how the passage of time may also affect stakeholders' perceptions.

Heathrow Terminal 5

The saga of T5 covers many years and many stages. For simplicity this description is broken into three stages:

1. The Egan era: construction of the terminal begins for British Airport Authority (BAA), supported by enlightened contractual arrangements.

2. BAA is sold to Ferrovial.

3. British Airways (BA) moves into the facility and begins operation.

STAGE 1 – THE EGAN ERA

The £4.3 billon Heathrow T5 project included a new terminal and satellite building, nine new tunnels, river diversions and road connections to the M25. It was hailed in 2006 as enlightened due to the adoption of innovative project management practices to avert the consequences of the traditional approach used in the UK construction industry. This traditional approach for a project of this size would potentially have resulted in average time overruns of two years, 40 per cent budget overruns and six to eight fatalities, whereas T5 had been completed on time and within budget at the human cost of two fatalities.

Under the unique T5 agreement, BAA absorbed total risk in all contracts for the project, and developed the concept of integrated teams reflecting a partnering relationship. This pioneering approach concentrated on early risk mitigation to anticipate, manage and reduce risks associated with the project. This change in BAA's culture was described as a 'watershed' (Potts, 2006), creating an environment for early problem-solving, sharing of information and collaboration. One example of this approach was the offsite prefabrication of the terminal's roof to minimise some of the risk of its advanced design.

The T5 project made extensive use of off-site trials and testing generating major cost and time savings during construction. Part of the roof and façade for the main terminal building was constructed in the Yorkshire countryside to ensure thorough testing before assembly on site took place. This allowed any problems to be revealed at an early stage, and the lessons learned applied to the construction and fit-out of the T5's 21 bays. 'Good engineering has been as important as good design in achieving a series of major buildings where on-site restrictions have severely limited the nature of the approach adopted.'[2]

STAGE 2 – BAA IS SOLD TO FERROVIAL

In June 2006, BAA was bought by a consortium led by Ferrovial, the Spanish construction company, and in August was officially delisted from the London Stock Exchange. On its website, Ferrovial describes itself as one of the leading private-sector developers of transport infrastructure. With the purchase of BAA, the airports it managed included Heathrow, Stansted, Glasgow, Edinburgh and

---

2   Publication of Architect Richard Rogers Partnership (now Rogers, Stirk, Harbour + Partners): see www.richardrogers.co.uk. The firm received a Royal Institute of British Architects (RIBA) London award in June 2008 for this building.

Belfast City. A large part of its business interests are now (at the time of writing) in airport management.[3]

Ferrovial borrowed US$18 billion to purchase BAA, and has been reported as 'struggling' to service this debt (Done 2008). The resulting cost-cutting activities included:

- replacement of many director-level staff with a new (Ferrovial) team to 'improve performance of Heathrow';[4]

- threats to reduce staff numbers in BAA's capital projects division;

- reluctance to use the 'T5 agreement' on future projects (Sweet 2008).

There may be some connection between the management culture of the new owner, its reported cost-cutting and the quality of T5 facilities when British Airways (BA) began operation in March 2008.[5]

STAGE 3 – THE OPENING

T5 was designed exclusively for BA's use, providing an opportunity to define specific business processes during the design and construction of a new terminal. On their website[6] BA lists aspects of the new terminal including:

- seamless check-in, designed to eliminate queuing;

- improvements in punctuality and baggage because nearly all BA flights arrive and depart from one terminal;

- state-of-the-art baggage system designed specifically for T5 using proven technology already in use at a number of global airports.

T5 was officially opened on 14 March, 2008 by HM Queen Elizabeth and began operating on 27 March, 2008. From the first day flights had to be cancelled, passengers were stranded, and over 15,000 pieces of baggage were lost. What

---

3   See www.BAA.com
4   See www.ft.com May 13, 2008 'BAA replaces Heathrow chief' – Kevin Done.
5   Some informal discussions with individuals connected to the UK construction industry.
6   http://www.terminal5.ba.com, accessed 30 April, 2008.

went wrong? The House of Commons Transport Committee published the report *The Opening of Heathrow Terminal 5* in November 2008. Both the report itself and the oral and written evidence support the information that was published in the media at the time of T5's opening.[7]

In July 2007 the terminal was reported as ready with testing on the check-in process and baggage systems being planned. BA management were to take possession of the building mid-September 2007, to test all the facilities and to ensure delivery of the new 'passenger-oriented experience'.

The CEO of BA, Willie Walsh, was interviewed by *The Times* on the day before T5 opened.[8] His positive and confident approach in answering questions about T5's readiness was interpreted (after the event) as hubris: '... he didn't countenance failure before the event, risking this over-confident interview ... our hunch is that he may be so determined, so driven, he simply does not recognise that incompetence could exist in those below him.'

In another interview, Walsh said:

> *T5 chaos was in part the result of calculated risk taken by the airline's management.... The company had known there were problems with the building from September when BA began to move in its staff and test systems. It was not 100 per cent complete... managers had reviewed their decision to open as planned on March 27 on a weekly basis and had decided that the problems caused by delaying the move to [October]... would be greater than those caused by pressing ahead.*[9]

Staff arriving for the first shifts at T5 were delayed by a number of issues:[10]

- There was a scarcity of specially designated staff car parking facilities, with the staff overflow car parks closed.

- There were delays in passing through security.

---

7   *The Opening of Heathrow Terminal 5*. House of Commons Transport Committee Report C 543, published November 3, 2008. Accessed 3 July 2009 at http://www.publications.parliament.uk/pa/cm200708.

8   business.timesonline.co.uk 'How hubris shut Willie Walsh's eyes to Heathrow catastrophe', March 29, 2008, Alice Miles and Helen Rumbelow.

9   business.timesonline.co.uk 'Airline tie-ups loom as crunch hits', May 18, 2008, Dominic O'Connell.

10 www.bbc.co.uk 'What went wrong at Heathrow's T5?' 31 March, 2008.

- Staff were unfamiliar with the new terminal building and the new systems.

- Baggage handlers claimed that they had not been adequately trained and did not have any support or backup even on this first day.

- BA asked for volunteers to make up additional numbers to provide this support, but due to low morale staff were not prepared to volunteer on their day off.

- Staff were not familiar with the new resource allocation system and therefore did not know what tasks they had been given on that day.

- Check-in staff continued to add bags to the system, causing the new baggage handling system to overload, because baggage handlers were not removing them quickly enough off the belts.

An Analysis

CONSTRUCTION OF THE TERMINAL

The construction of the terminal was lauded as a success, from a time, cost, scope and quality perspective, but also from the management of risk and reduction of disputes and conflicts. Perhaps BAA and BA management were indulging in the 'halo effect' – the construction project went so well, the implementation would also go equally well.

STAFF PREPARATION

The reports from staff of inadequate training show a lack of understanding of the importance of training and adequate preparation for implementation. There was no contingency on that first day, no recognition that something might go wrong:

- Management did not ask staff to come early to counter potential delays in entering a building they had not entered before.

- They did not pay for additional staff, merely asking staff to come in on their day off to help out.

- The baggage handlers were unfamiliar with the new technology and processes

- The staff were unclear on their assignments for that first day because they did not know how to use the new resource management system.

- The baggage handling system appeared to have no backup system to support the new complex system.

What does the experience of the T5 construction project and its implementation tell us about success and failure? BA's reputation is damaged from the events of T5's opening. It did indeed fail on opening, but the failure was clearly a failure to manage the people side – poor preparation of the people responsible for operation of the facility. If T5's success were to be judged just on the completion of the construction project it would continue to be known as a success. But for now T5 is synonymous with failure, because of the poor management of the implementation of the outcome of the project. The perception of the travelling public and many other stakeholders is that T5 'does not work'. BA recognised that they must alter such a perception and have begun a campaign on their website (www. BA.com) of regularly promoting improvements in service and efficiency of their operations.

It will be interesting to see how T5 is perceived in five to ten years. Australia's best known building, the Sydney Opera House, was perceived as a 'white elephant' and an 'acoustic and aesthetic disaster' when it first opened in 1973 (Murray 2004). It is now regarded as the most recognisable tourist destination in Australia: no-one would describe it as a failure today!

This chapter has focused on research of failure and success, and then used the example of the construction and implementation of the T5 facilities at Heathrow to show that success does not just depend on delivering the agreed functionality of the outcome on time, within budget. To reduce the chances of failure and increase the chances of success, attention to the needs and expectations of a wide group of stakeholders is essential. From the perspective of the T5 example, many different stakeholders had many different needs and expectations. These expectations include:

- the UK Government's need to revive the reputation of the UK construction industry through implementation of the Egan Report;

- Ferrovial's needs to realise their investment in purchasing BAA;

- BA's needs for an iconic home at Heathrow;

- BA's customers' need for trouble-free travel;

- BA's staff's need for tools and processes to do their job.

The differing perceptions of the success of T5 would vary enormously depending on who was asked to comment, which part of the whole of the T5 work – construction project, implementation or operation – was being examined, and also at what time relative to the disastrous opening of T5 the question was asked and answered.

The next chapter will discuss the concept of stakeholders in organisational activities. It will trace the history of the development of the idea and purpose of stakeholders. Stakeholders are defined and a structured methodology is introduced. This methodology can be used to identify important stakeholders, and to understand and manage their expectations for the purpose of building and maintaining essential relationships between the stakeholder community and the organisation.

2

Who can be Stakeholders?

In the previous chapter, an analysis of the opening of Heathrow Terminal 5 (T5) in April 2008 showed that the public's perception of its failure persists despite all British Airways' (BA) efforts to change this view. T5 is perceived by the public to be a disaster because of the chaos of its first week of operation.[1] The *perception* of failure of the whole project is the result of the poorly planned implementation: a result, in part, of the failure of BA management to prepare staff for operating in the new terminal.

This chapter will focus on the development of the ***Stakeholder*** *Circle* methodology as a set of *processes and practices* to guide organisations in the development of the *essential relationships* necessary for the achievement of their *business strategies*. The first section discusses the emergence of the concept of stakeholders and the importance of the relationship between stakeholder and organisation. The second section explores the activities that an organisation may perform to achieve its business strategies and objectives, and the nature of the relationships with its stakeholder community. The third section will discuss essential aspects of stakeholders: the definition, a discussion of the 'stakes' that a stakeholder may have. The final section discusses the emergence of the ***Stakeholder*** *Circle* methodology from the research and experience of myself and colleagues.

The Emergence of the Concept of Stakeholders

THEORIES OF STAKEHOLDERS

Theories of stakeholders have been constructed in terms of the relationship between an organisation and its stakeholders. Freeman, (1984) is credited with

---

1   My personal experience of T5 on several trips in the months after the opening is that the facilities worked well. I was able to transfer from an international flight to a UK domestic flight with the minimum of trouble.

the development of the foundation definition of stakeholders as 'any group or individual who can affect or is affected by the achievement of the organisation's objectives'.

Stakeholder theory has developed views of the importance of stakeholders and how stakeholder management or engagement contributes to the success of organisational activities. Organisational wealth can be created (or destroyed) through relationships with its stakeholders. In developing processes and practices for stakeholder management and engagement, successful organisations understand how far key stakeholders will go to achieve, promote, or protect their stake. Just as important to organisation success is the understanding of what will need to be done to ensure the best relationships between the organisation, its activities and the contribution needed from stakeholders for those activities to be successful.

WHO ARE STAKEHOLDERS?

Stakeholders may be groups or individuals who supply critical resources, or place something of value at risk through their investment of funds, career or time in pursuit of the organisation's business strategies or goals. Alternatively, stakeholders may be groups or individuals opposed to the organisation or some aspect of its activities. Stakeholders are defined as 'individuals or groups who will be impacted by, or can influence the success or failure of an organisation's activities'.

WHAT IS AT STAKE?

By definition, a stakeholder has a stake in the activity. This stake may be:

- an interest;

- rights (legal or moral);

- ownership;

- contribution in the form of knowledge or support.

It is important to consider the nature of a stakeholder's stake when defining a stakeholder's requirements, or defining how the individual or group can impact the organisation's activities. Definitions of stake are summarised in Table 2.1.

Table 2.1   Stake defined

Interest	A person or group of persons is affected by a decision related to the activity or its outcomes: • effect of street closures for a public event; • support for the creation of a nature park in another country or region.

Rights	To be treated in a certain way or to have a particular right protected:
	• legal right:
	   – occupational health and safety, privacy.
	• moral right:
	   – heritage protection activists, environmentalists.

Ownership	A circumstance when a person or group of persons has a legal title to an asset or a property: • resumption of personal or business property for road works; • intellectual property; • shareholders' 'ownership' in an organisation.
Knowledge	Specialist knowledge or organisational knowledge required to enable the activity.

Impact or influence	Stakeholders may be:
	• impacted by the activity or its outcomes:
	   – staff, customers, shareholders.
	• impact (or influence) on the activity or its outcomes:
	   – sponsor, governments (legislation, regulation), the public.

Contribution	Stakeholders who are responsible for: • supply of resources; – people, material, funding. • advocacy for objectives or activity success, buffer between organisation and activity teams or the performance of the activity.

Interest

An interest is a circumstance in which a person or group will be affected by a decision, action or outcome. An example of interest is to consider a public event, such as a major sporting contest, being conducted in a residential area. For the time that event is running and also over the time it takes to set it up and take it down, the residents will have an interest in that event, even if they are not interested in that particular sport.

Rights

Rights can be either legal or moral rights.

- Legal rights cover the legal claim of a group or individual to be treated in a certain way or to have a particular right protected. Legal rights are usually enshrined in a country's legislation; examples include privacy laws and occupational health and safety.

- Moral rights cover moral issues that may affect large groups of people or natural phenomena, such as environmental, heritage or social issues. Social issues may extend to speaking on behalf of countries or individuals who cannot speak for themselves or defend themselves and encompass both the activists and the 'victims'. Moral rights are usually not covered by legislation. It is moral rights such as the ones described here that organisations may address in corporate social responsibility (CSR) activities.

Ownership

Most stakeholders will have an interest, many will have rights. Many individuals will also have a stake of ownership, such as:

- a worker's right to earn their living from their knowledge;

- shareholders' ownership of a portion of an organisation's assets;

- intellectual property resulting from the exploitation of an idea;

- legal title to an asset or a property.

Knowledge

A team member or employee who applies experience or knowledge to the production of an asset for an organisation will be making a contribution to the organisation's activity. This knowledge is important to the organisation's success, but as discussed earlier, the employee or team member will be impacted by the success or failure of the activity.

Contribution

The contribution that a stakeholder may make to the activity falls into the following categories:

- Allocation of resources – this can be people or materials.

- Provision of funds – either the initial approval or ongoing assurance of continued funding.

- Knowledge or experience essential for successful achievement of the objectives of the activity.

Knowledge of the stake that a stakeholder may have in the success or failure of the activity will be important information for managing the relationship between the work of the activity and stakeholders. To clarify the nature of this relationship and to further develop the concept of 'who can be stakeholders?' and 'why are they important?' it is important to discuss the various assumptions, frameworks and definitions of the nature of any relationship between an organisation, its activities and its stakeholders.

UNDERLYING ASSUMPTIONS AND FRAMEWORKS

The work of Stoney and Winstanley (2001) is useful for exploring ways that stakeholder relationships can be defined. Five dimensions to describe the various stakeholder management approaches are:

1. political perspectives;

2. purpose and objectives of considering stakeholders;

3. value of considering stakeholders;

4. considering stakeholder intervention levels;

5. degree of stakeholder enforcement.

They are summarised in Table 2.2 and Figure 2.1.

Dimension 1 – political perspectives of stakeholders

At one extreme lies the Marxist view of political struggle between capital and labour: this view rejects the stakeholder concept. At the other end of that continuum lies the *unitarists* who believe that shareholders, as owners of capital, will be most important in terms of authenticity of their claims on the organisation. The position adopted during the development of the *Stakeholder Circle* methodology is indicated by the shaded dot in Figure 2.1. This is a pluralist perspective recognising that there is a diverse range of stakeholders with valid claims to consider. This position, and the positions developed in the other dimensions are described in detail in Walker, Bourne and Shelley (2008).

Table 2.2   Summary of stakeholder theories and Bourne's position

Dimension	Continuum End position 1	Continuum End position 2	Bourne position	Stakeholder focus
1: political perspective	Marxist: rejects SH* concept – cynical exercise in worker control.	Unitarian: authenticity of claims on the organisation: primacy of SH.	Pluralist: accommodation of multiple interests.	Shareholders AND workers Wide range of potential SHs.
2: implementing stakeholder concepts	Reform: regulations to institutionalise SH concepts.	Analysis: power, access and influence and appropriate management within SH community.	Pragmatic: all appropriate SH relationships to manage the community.	Wide range of SHs identified as having a stake in the activity and analysis of power, access and influence.
3: value of stakeholder engagement	Instrumental: SHs are instruments and agents whose power must be harnessed and controlled.	Intrinsic: having moral rights for their needs to be considered.	More intrinsic than instrumental.	Recognition of SHs who have moral rights to be addressed.
4: power to intervene	Regulation: community's right through regulations at local, regional, national or global. level	Individualism: consideration of the individual's intrinsic rights.	Governance: SH engagement considered as corporate governance issue.	Assess the influence and power that all SHs may have and plan to manage. relationships
5: stakeholder enforcement	Voluntary and ethical action on the part of SHs and team members.	Coercion: a plan MUST be enacted as formulated; legal rights enforced.	Best practice: connection between SH engagement and business practice.	Collaboration and mutuality.

* SH = stakeholder

Dimension 2 – purpose and objectives of considering stakeholders

This continuum ranges from reform through regulations on how valid stakeholders should be recognised and treated at one end to analysis at the other. Mapping of stakeholder interest lies at the analysis end of that continuum, derived from the analysis of stakeholders to understand and manage their power, access and influence within that community. The *Stakeholder Circle*

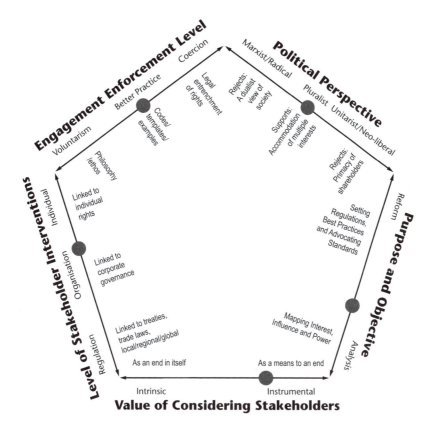

Figure 2.1   Five approaches to stakeholder management

methodology supports pragmatic intervention in stakeholder relationships to manage the outcomes of an organisation's activities most effectively.

Dimension 3 – value of considering stakeholders

This dimension derives a continuum of instrumentality at one end – stakeholders are instruments and agents whose power must be harnessed and controlled; and at the other end as intrinsically having moral rights for their needs to be considered.

The *Stakeholder Circle* methodology favours instrumentality through recognising a need to understand a stakeholder's value proposition and, through this understanding, the development of a more appropriate engagement strategy for organisational success. However, it is also essential to recognise that stakeholders' moral needs should be considered. As CSR becomes a more common mode driver of organisational activity, this (intrinsic) value will contribute to more successful delivery of organisational strategies and goals.

Dimension 4 – considering the stakeholders' intervention level

For this category, the continuum spreads from the concept of the community's right to intervene through regulations at local government, regional, national or global level. At the other end of the spectrum lies the individual's intrinsic right to intervene. The organisation is positioned at the mid-point, where it can benefit from understanding what influence and power stakeholders may have and can plan and negotiate to influence plans and actions of the stakeholder community. This position implies a need for stakeholder engagement and integration into planning, communication planning and risk management of all organisational activities.

Dimension 5 – considering the degree of stakeholder enforcement

This final dimension relates to the way in which stakeholder interests may be institutionalised within an engagement plan. The extreme positions are voluntary action on the part of stakeholders and team members and coercion where a plan must be enacted as formulated. The processes and practices supporting increasing maturity in stakeholder management and engagement should be built through communication of the connection between focus on stakeholder engagement and business practice.

Organisation Activities and Stakeholder Communities

The description of the five dimensions of stakeholder management and engagement provides a foundation for developing views on how to effectively manage stakeholder relationships for each activity that an organisation undertakes. It also provides a starting point for recognising the diverse activities an organisation must perform, and therefore the diverse stakeholder communities and relationships it must maintain. Consequently, it is not possible to identify a standard set of stakeholders for the organisation: every activity that an organisation undertakes will have its own unique set of stakeholders.

Depending on the type of activity and even on the different stages or phases of that activity there will be variation in the membership of the stakeholder community. Activities that an organisation may undertake can include the following:

- corporate social responsibility (CSR) activities;

- competitive advantage;

- governance;

- improving the bottom line;

- mergers and acquisitions (M&A);

- business change;

- projects and programmes of work.

CORPORATE SOCIAL RESPONSIBILITY (CSR)

CSR is defined as the responsibility of an organisation towards stakeholders (individual or groups) who may be overlooked or unfairly treated in the *shareholder value* model of organisational management. It seeks to redress past situations where large numbers of voiceless stakeholders had been ignored, while organisations pursued short-term strategies aimed at ensuring that shareholders maintained their dividends. The environment, other (less fortunate) countries or their inhabitants will generally fall within the purview of social responsibility.

An organisation's employees may often be included in this category, particularly when the organisation reduces expenditure (and headcount) in the interests of shareholder value. Employees can be greatly affected by success or failure of the firm, have invested in the organisation (skills and experience), are financially dependent on the success of the organisation, and are often dependent on their workplace for social relationships, self-identity and self-actualisation: the company has duties to employees.

COMPETITOR ANALYSIS

Organisations operating in competitive industries will benefit from frequent analysis of their competitors within a similar framework to stakeholder analysis. Competitors are actually stakeholders because their actions, or even presence in the market, will affect the organisation's ability to realise its business strategies.

GOVERNANCE

Corporate governance is essential for an organisation to achieve its business strategies and objectives through:

- building effective mechanisms for making investment decisions;

- monitoring and measurement of the implementation and effectiveness of these decisions;

- management of strategic risk;

- ensuring the proper and efficient use of the organisation's resources.

Within the corporate governance framework, stakeholder analysis will be a crucial responsibility to ensure that all appropriate relationships are understood and managed. While shareholders and the leadership of the organisation are obvious candidates, a full stakeholder analysis may reveal other individuals or groups who have stakes in the organisation that cannot be ignored.

IMPROVING THE BOTTOM LINE

There is evidence that organisations that are committed to stakeholder engagement experience an improvement to their bottom line. Collins and Porras (1995) report on research that indicated that companies that invest heavily in employee training, knowledge transfer and alignment of organisational values, have outperformed comparable companies by an average of 15 times. Organisations can improve their bottom line by responding to stakeholder concerns. Stakeholder groups whose issues must be addressed include:

- employees:

  - HR and industrial;

  - diversity issues.

- community:

  - heritage;

  - environmental;

  - fairness.

MERGERS AND ACQUISITIONS (M&A)

The joining of organisations either by way of a 'friendly' merger, or a more hostile acquisition of one organisation by another inevitably results in disruption to the business. Attempts to form a new structure and culture from the merged organisations can be hindered by misunderstandings or the resistance of employees. Key to successful management of these disruptions is a clear understanding of all those who have a stake in the outcome, their power to influence and obstruct, as well as their rights, obligations, and interests. Attention to all stakeholders affected by the transition and ensuring that the needs and expectations of the key stakeholders are understood and their perceptions managed allows the newly merged organisation to re-establish efficient operations with less delay.

INTERNAL BUSINESS CHANGE PROGRAMMES

Business change programmes, either as a result of M&A, or because the organisation decides to restructure to meet some competitive or market need, will cause disruption to the business. This disruption may be caused by stakeholders' reaction to uncertainty, resistance to change, fear of redundancy, or striving for power in the new environment. Organisations can reduce these disruptions through targeted communication, inclusion of stakeholders in decision-making, and measuring effectiveness of the communication and also of the change itself.

PROJECTS AND PROGRAMMES OF WORK

Projects and programmes need to understand and maintain stakeholder relationships throughout the course of the project or programme. Managing the expectations and therefore perceptions of stakeholders will ensure best level of support from supportive stakeholders and reduce the resistance of unsupportive stakeholders, assisting the delivery of the outcomes. A generally supportive stakeholder community will assist in achieving improvements in delivery through adherence to schedule or budget. These improvements will in turn benefit the organisation through a reduction in numbers of projects not completed, or at the very least a reduction in projects that go over time and over budget.

The Development of the *Stakeholder Circle* Methodology

The *Stakeholder Circle* methodology has been developed from many sources. Starting with my own experiences, the concepts of the methodology have built on the research of others and been refined by feedback from clients, colleagues and students who have attended my training workshops or conference presentations. Table 2.3 summarises a selection of methodologies developed by individuals, companies, universities and government bodies for stakeholder identification and management that have formed the foundation for the *Stakeholder* Circle methodology.

The concepts of *power, legitimacy and urgency* (Mitchell, Agle and Wood 1997) are valuable for identifying important stakeholders. Development of

Table 2.3   Some stakeholder management methodologies

Methodology	Individual, Group or Organisation	Comments
Definition of categories of stakeholders.	(Savage, Nix, Whitehead and Blair 1991) (Mitchell, Agle and Wood 1997)	Four generic types – supportive, mixed blessing, non-supportive, marginal. Eight-part stakeholder typology based on assessments of the strengths of three attributes: power, legitimacy and urgency.
Comprehensive stakeholder identification, assessment and engagement.	(Briner, Hastings and Geddes 1996)	Focus on communication as important part of stakeholder management.
Focus on enhancing economic value and organisational wealth as well as recording what stakeholders require from the project.	(Fletcher, Guthrie, Steane, Roos and Pike 2003) (Frooman 1999)	A process for mapping stakeholder expectations based on value hierarchies and Key Performance Areas (KPA). An analysis of ways organisations can plan their stakeholder management strategies, rather than response strategies.
Stakeholder Circle® visualisation tool and methodology.	(Bourne 2008)	Continual process for identification, prioritisation, engagement strategy for developing long-term relationships.

appropriate engagement strategies has built on the work of Briner, Hastings and Geddes (1996); Frooman (1999); and Fletcher, Guthrie, Steane, Roos and Pike (2003).

The extensions of existing methodologies are:

- The idea that the stakeholder community is dynamic not static: as the activity moves through its phases and with the passage of time the membership of the community will change. This change may be triggered by changes in the leadership or the organisation or stakeholder group, or changes in the environment, changes in the perception of the wider community, or operational changes in the work itself. To track these changes the practice of regular reviews of the stakeholder community and the attitude of key stakeholders to the activity itself has been included.

- *Mutuality*: the two-way nature of a relationship requires recognition of why each stakeholder has been selected to be a stakeholder, but also what the stakeholder requires from the success or failure of the activity in question, i.e., their expectations. Expectation (or perception) management is a keystone for success of this methodology: knowing a stakeholder's expectations means that communication can be directed to meet their requirements or seek to modify their expectations. Communication plans will consider expectations as the key to designing an appropriate message as well as selecting the best messenger.

- The use of a consistent framework of ratings for understanding the essential aspects of stakeholders as members of a dynamic community. The ratings allow the team making the analysis and managing the relationship to negotiate and document elements of the relationship between the activity and their community in a consistent way. The ratings are based on three sets of attributes:

  1. *Power*: the power to cause permanent change to the activity, to stop it, to cause a change of direction at the high end, or to having no power over the activity at all, at the low end.

2.   *Proximity:* a measure of the closeness of the stakeholder to the activity. Full time team members are rated high, while senior leadership team members or members of the public are rated low for proximity even if they have been rated high for *power*.

3.   *Urgency:* a measure of the importance of the activity or its outcomes to the stakeholder and a measure of how much the stakeholder is prepared to act to achieve this outcome. *Urgency* is divided into two sub-categories: *value* and *action*.

- The consistency of the rating mechanisms also supports the ability of the methodology to measure the effectiveness of the stakeholder engagement efforts through measuring changes within the stakeholder community over time.

The *Stakeholder Circle*

The *Stakeholder Circle* methodology is based on the concept that an organisation's activities to achieve its business strategies and objectives are central to any consideration of the stakeholder community that the activity's success depends on. Figure 2.2 shows these relationships. All decisions or understanding of the relationships is from the perspective of the manager of the activity. Surrounding the activity itself is the team, often overlooked in many stakeholder engagement processes. Surrounding the team is the community of stakeholders that has been identified as being key to the success of the activity *at the present time*. The outmost circle references potential stakeholders: those who may, or will, be important to the success of the activity at a later stage.

By differentiating between current stakeholders and potential stakeholders in this way, confusion about which stakeholders are important at that moment and how best to manage the current relationships will be minimised, while ensuring that planning for future relationships is managed effectively. The stakeholders in the outer circle may also be considered in risk management planning because they may cause the activity to be at risk of failure in the future, or these stakeholders may need to be considered in an organisation's marketing plans, as potential customers.

Figure 2.2   **The relationships within the** *Stakeholder* *Circle*

MANAGING STAKEHOLDER RELATIONSHIPS

The **Stakeholder** *Circle* is a five-step methodology that provides a flexible approach to understanding and managing relationships within and around the activity. It also supports the concept of the dynamic nature of the stakeholder community. The methodology is based on the concept that an activity can only exist with the informed consent of its stakeholder community, and that managing the relationships between this community and the activity will increase the chances of success. The stakeholder community consists of individuals and groups, each with a different potential to influence the activity's outcome positively or negatively. The categorisation and charting of important stakeholders' ability to influence the project's success or failure holds the key to targeting the right stakeholders at the right time during the life of the activity. Through this analysis the team will develop appreciation of the right level of engagement, i.e., the information and communication needed to influence stakeholders' perceptions, expectations and actions.

The **Stakeholder** *Circle* is a flexible model that can be adjusted to cater for changes in stakeholder community membership and stakeholder influence throughout the life of the activity. There are five steps to the methodology:

- step 1: identification of all stakeholders;

- step 2: prioritisation to determine who is important;

- step 3: visualisation to understand the overall stakeholder community;

- step 4: engagement through effective communications;

- step 5: monitoring the effect of the engagement.

SOFTWARE SUPPORT FOR THE METHODOLOGY

Software can support an organisation's management of its stakeholder relationships through the ability to maintain a history of stakeholder relationship management, to simplify information-gathering about stakeholders and their attitudes to the work of the organisation, to enable more effective monitoring and measurement of communication effectiveness and finally to gather data to support predictive risk and stakeholder analysis.

There are a number of options for software support of the process. These options will be described in more detail in Chapter 4. They are described briefly below:

- The simplest option is a word template – the *stakeholder-on-a-page* (SOAP). This MS Word template gathers data from multiple reviews for each stakeholder. The information about each stakeholder is captured and retained to allow for trends in the relationship to be viewed and used for analysis where necessary.

- A spreadsheet which can perform calculations and produce simple graphics for reporting on progress of stakeholder relationship management may be the best option for an organisation (SWS).

- A database (SIMS) that can support complex data collection, sophisticated reporting and analysis.

Whatever the origin or capability of the software, an organisation that seriously intends to understand and manage stakeholder relationships affecting its work should move to software support once the methodology has been proven and accepted by senior management, either by developing bespoke systems tailored to each organisation's specific needs or by implementing an existing tool.

Conclusion

This chapter described the development of the *Stakeholder* Circle methodology, through a discussion of the origins of the concept of stakeholder first raised in the 1960s, and a description of the many frameworks driving how an organisation might approach management of its stakeholders. The application of ideas of stakeholder management and relationships between the organisation and its stakeholder community led to an examination of the different types of activities an organisation may perform to achieve its business strategies and objectives. Finally, the methodologies and work of other researchers were explored as the foundation of the *Stakeholder* Circle methodology.

Chapter 3 describes in detail the first two steps of the methodology with instructions on how to use the methodology to assist the organisation to understand, build and maintain the essential relationships with its stakeholders.

SECTION II

Guidebook

The *Stakeholder Circle* methodology and its theoretical framework were described in Section I, Chapters 1 and 2. For those who are seeking to use this book as a set of procedures to improve stakeholder management and engagement practices in an organisation, Section II, Chapters 3–6 can be used as a stand-alone guidebook.

The Right Stakeholders

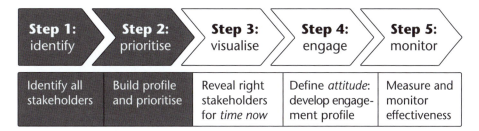

Step 1: identify	Step 2: prioritise	Step 3: visualise	Step 4: engage	Step 5: monitor
Identify all stakeholders	Build profile and prioritise	Reveal right stakeholders for *time now*	Define *attitude*: develop engage-ment profile	Measure and monitor effectiveness

Figure 3.1   Chapter 3 focus

The graphic that heads this chapter is intended to assist in designing the appropriate approach to managing stakeholder relationships in organisations. Similar graphics will head Chapters 4, 5 and 6. When implementing the methodology it is not essential to start at *step 1*; different *steps* of the methodology can be selected as discussed in Section III of this book, depending on an organisation's readiness to implement stakeholder management processes and practices.

The identification of stakeholders is the first stage of a continuous process to collect the information needed to build a profile of each stakeholder, for the purpose of effective communication. Every step of the *Stakeholder Circle* methodology focuses on gathering, confirming or modifying this key information about stakeholders. Figure 3.1 shows the structured approach for data collection in each of the *steps* of the methodology.

Step 1: Identify

The essential first step in managing stakeholder relationships is to know who the stakeholders are. *Step 1: identify* in the **Stakeholder** Circle methodology provides a course of action for:

- knowing who stakeholders are for a particular time – *time now*.

- gathering information about each individual or group identified as stakeholders, in anticipation of planning targeted communication.

Step 1: identify consists of three activities:

1. developing a list of stakeholders;

2. identifying *mutuality*:

    a. how each stakeholder is important to the work;

    b. what each stakeholder expects from success (or failure) of the work;

3. categorising: documenting each stakeholder's:

    a. *directions of influence:* these are *upwards, downwards, outwards,* and *sidewards;*

    b. relationship to the organisation – whether they are *internal* to the organisation or *external.*

The output of this step will be a list of *all* stakeholders that fit the definition of stakeholder: *individuals or groups who are impacted by, or can impact, the work or its outcomes at this particular time in the lifecycle of the work.*

1. DEVELOP THE STAKEHOLDER LIST

Developing the stakeholder list requires two actions:

1. Select a team for identification and analysis of the stakeholder community. Box 3.1 describes the selection process and discusses the importance of teams for understanding and managing stakeholder relationships.

2. Assemble information about stakeholders (this is often accomplished through brainstorming):[1]

---

1   The stakeholder list is most often developed through a brainstorming process, where members of the team contribute names of groups or individuals that meet the specifications of the definition.

> **BOX 3.1 THE IMPORTANCE OF TEAMS**
>
> This team will ideally consist of 3 to 5 members, including:
>
> 1. The project manager or manager of the work;
>
> 2. Some core team members;
>
> 3. Someone who understands the power structures and politics of the organisation, preferably the sponsor or a senior manager of the organisation.
>
> If possible, membership of this (stakeholder relationship management) team should remain constant over the entire time that the work is being undertaken. Maintaining consistency of membership of this team provides some assurance of reduced subjectivity in decisions made about the stakeholder community and its membership.
>
> An additional benefit to using teams for identification of stakeholders is the sharing of the knowledge that each team member has about certain stakeholders or the stakeholder community, and thus adding to the knowledge that each team member has about the stakeholder community and the power structures of the organisation.
>
> Data collected through a classroom exercise comparing the efficiency of team and individuals in decision-making included in Successful Stakeholder Management (PMI Seminars World Series 2006 and 2007) workshops, shows that of approximately 500 participants, only 6 individuals scored better than their team.

a. information about their influence on the team and the progress of the work, or influence on the achievement of outcomes;

b. *mutuality*: what they require from success or failure of the work (expectations) and their influence on the work (why they are stakeholders).

How many stakeholders?

Some organisational activities are large and complex, and may affect many stakeholders. For example, construction of public facilities or national infrastructure projects will affect private citizens, landowners, and the natural and historical environment. In a case such as this, it is essential to recognise and accept that there will be large numbers of stakeholders to be identified. There is often an unconscious boundary on what a 'good number' of stakeholders can be; it is important for the team and for their management to understand that while the initial number of stakeholders identified may appear unwieldy or overwhelming, *step 2: prioritise* provides a structured and logical means to prioritise the key stakeholders for the current time. If a large number of stakeholders have been identified, or it is expected that this will occur, it may be necessary to conduct the identification and prioritisation workshops at different times. Generally

---

BOX 3.2   ITERATIONS OF DATA COLLECTIONS AND REVIEWS

Gathering information about stakeholders may require a number of iterations. The process is continuous with the information assembled over time. The team should not expect to be able to answer all the essential questions about the stakeholder community even with the assistance of the sponsor, or a senior manager who knows how the culture of the organisation works and knows about the most important stakeholders. It is not acceptable to make guesses about stakeholders' preferences, expectations, or attitudes. Any assumptions about stakeholders or their place in the stakeholder community must be tested and validated. Also important to recognise is that the expectations and attitudes of stakeholders identified in this process may change over time.

---

three-hour sessions are optimal – given the amount of detailed analysis that needs to occur for effective gathering of essential information. Box 3.2 above describes the importance of iterative data collections and reviews.

2. IDENTIFY *MUTUALITY*

Mutuality adds an additional dimension for describing the nature of relationships. Table 3.1 summarises the different levels of relationships that can exist in an organisation. The application of *mutuality* to stakeholder relationship management recognises both the maturity of the relationship and the two-way nature of any relationship whether personal, family or work-related. The team has identified stakeholders who can impact its success or are impacted by the outcomes of the work. However, the identification of individuals or groups who can affect the success or failure of the work or its outcomes is only part of the task. Two questions must be asked to gauge and then document both characteristics of each stakeholder:

1.   'How is this stakeholder important to us? What is their stake?'

Table 3.1   Summary of the relationship model of French and Granrose (1995)

Level		Nature of relationship
Mutuality	Most mature	A partnership where both parties recognise and practice in an environment that is mutually beneficial; best described as a trusting/trustworthy relationship.
Reciprocity	Common	A 'give and take' relationship, such as exchange of favours, commonly practiced in a business environment.
Exploitation	Basic	Taking advantage: describes unequal power relations.

2.   'What does this stakeholder require from the success or failure of the work's execution or its outcomes?'

The answers to these questions form the basis of defining and developing a mutual relationship between the stakeholder community and the team. The information obtained in this way is then applied to the list of stakeholders developed from the stakeholder identification exercise.

The stakeholder's importance

The answer to the first question establishes that this person or group actually is a stakeholder and what their potential contribution to the work's success (or failure) may be. Generally, a stakeholder is important to the work because he or she:

- is an important source of funds, personnel or materials;

- can impact the success or failure of the project through either action or inaction.

The stakeholder's expectations

The answer to the second question establishes the stakeholder's expectations, or requirements, from the success or failure of the project. Generally a stakeholder will have expectations of either personal or organisational gain through either the success or failure of a particular organisational activity. Table 3.2 provides

Table 3.2   Examples of stakeholder expectations

Expectations or requirements	Some examples
Personal gain	• enhanced power; • enhanced reputation; • career advancement; • monetary advantage – salary increase or performance bonus; • avoidance of negative consequences of the outcomes of the work; • a peaceful life.
Organisational gain (for the organisation as a whole or a department or group within the organisation)	• enhanced power; • enhanced reputation; • social recognition; • social integration – corporate social responsibility (CSR) compliance.

a list of examples of stakeholders' expectations that might be relevant to an organisation's activities.

Gathering data about mutuality

An understanding of the two parts of the relationship with the stakeholder community is crucial to subsequent steps in the stakeholder mapping process and to developing targeted communication strategies. However the questions may not be answered satisfactorily in the first workshop, and team members may need to assemble the necessary information over time, from a variety of sources. Sources for additional information about stakeholders' expectations or requirements can include:

- gathering information in the public record: web pages, Google information;

- organisational reports: Annual Report, business case, requirements documents;

- asking others who may have more information;

- asking the stakeholder;

- seeking confirmation of data collected from other sources, such as colleagues, who may have additional information about the stakeholder community being analysed.

Information about a stakeholder's expectations may also be acquired through surveys. Many organisations are now using Customer Satisfaction Surveys (CSS) as part of the project closure activities. An essential part of this CSS process is to get an early understanding of the expectations of stakeholders who will be surveyed later, to serve as a baseline for comparing final survey answers.

The final activity in *step 1: identify* is to categorise the listed stakeholders according to the type of influence that they can have on the work or its outcomes, or that the work and outcomes can hold over the stakeholders. This is the start of the refinement of the raw list of stakeholders into more manageable information. Box 3.3 provides some suggestions for ensuring that information gathered about expectations is as valid as possible.

BOX 3.3   'WHAT ARE YOUR EXPECTATIONS?'

While it makes sense to ask an individual about their expectations with regard to the work or its outcomes, this should not be the only source of information about this stakeholder. Sometimes people will provide information they think the team wants to hear, for politeness, or just to save time or effort. It is always a useful rule of thumb to seek data from at least two separate sources, to increase the accuracy and appropriateness of the information.

---

3. DIRECTIONS OF INFLUENCE

There are two sets of influence to consider:

1. Is the *direction of influence* of the stakeholder *upwards, downwards, outwards* or *sidewards?* These influences are shown in Figure 3.2.

2. Is the stakeholder part of the organisation or outside it: *internal* to the organisation or *external* to the organisation?

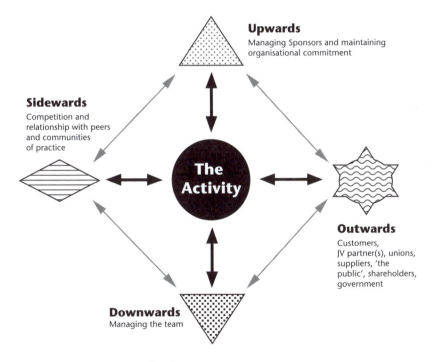

Figure 3.2   **Directions of influence**

Directions of influence defined

Upwards defines the influence that senior management, especially the sponsor, exerts over the activity. It is shown in the **Stakeholder** *Circle* colour mapping as orange.[2]

Downwards denotes team members, whether full-time staff, consultants, contractors or specialists who work with the manager to achieve the objectives or outcomes of the activity: teams or team members are shown as green. *Outwards* stakeholders are those outside the entity that does the work and will include individuals and groups such as end users, government, regulators, the public, shareholders and lobby groups: *outwards* stakeholders are shown as blue. Finally *sidewards* stakeholders are peers of the manager, industry groups and managers within the organisation who are considered to be at the same level professionally: *sidewards* stakeholders are shown as purple. Adding colour to the depiction of the stakeholder community can add an additional dimension; it can also be recorded simply as U for *upwards*, D for *downwards*, O for *outwards*, and S for *sidewards*.

Categorisations for *internal* and *external* are primarily directed to understanding the potential communication channels. Direct access in some form should be available to *internal* stakeholders, whereas *external* stakeholders may be more difficult to contact. The **Stakeholder** *Circle* software (SIMS) will cause the colours denoting the four directions to be light (for *external*) and dark (for *internal*). Otherwise these dimensions will be documented as E for *external* and I for *internal*.

COLLATING DATA ABOUT EACH STAKEHOLDER

The output of each step of the **Stakeholder** *Circle* methodology builds information about the stakeholder community that is essential for targeted communication. There are a number of ways to achieve this; they are described in detail in Chapter 4 and examples provided of their use:

- *Stakeholder-on-a-page*™, (SOAP) a document that can either be used in soft copy (MS Word) or hard copy to gather information about each stakeholder;

---

2   Colour coding provides an additional dimension to assist in mapping the complex stakeholder community: see Figure 4.10 for examples of the use of colour to provide additional information about the stakeholder community.

- Spreadsheet – Stakeholder WorkSheet (SWS);

- Stakeholder Information Management System (SIMS): a database that supports all steps of the methodology and stores and presents this data in graphics and project reports.[3]

The results of these activities will be a list of stakeholders, categorised according to their influence on the projects, with additional information collected about their importance to the work and their expectations of the outcomes of the work. This data is essential for the next step in stakeholder relationship management – *step 2: prioritise.*

Step 2: Prioritise

The list of stakeholders must now be further refined by:

- collecting additional data to further categorise and understand each stakeholder in the community;

- creating further opportunities for the team to investigate the relationships: it may not be possible to gather all necessary information on stakeholders the first time;

- a reduction in the subjective aspects of people making decisions about other people, by the provision of a set of consistent statements on which the team can base decisions about members of their stakeholder community;

- a consistent foundation for analysis and reporting on the relationships through trend analysis (it is important to compare like with like), once again the outcome from the use of these consistent statements;

- establishing a credible means to understand the relative importance of all stakeholders identified: documentation including comments recorded and even the evidence of the ratings themselves will add credibility to decisions about stakeholders that were previously an educated guess at best.

---

3   For more information on the ***Stakeholder*** *Circle* go to www.stakeholder-management.com

Most stakeholder management methodologies rely on an individual's (or the team's) subjective assessment of who is important: some of these methodologies were analysed in Chapter 2. The approach adopted in the *Stakeholder* Circle methodology attempts to provide consistency in decision-making about stakeholders. It does this by providing a structure to make decisions, within a framework used by the team members to discuss and agree on the relative importance of the stakeholders they have identified.

THE EFFECT OF CULTURE

An organisation's culture will often drive a focus on certain types of stakeholders, and not on others. For example, some organisations will consider shareholders as the most important stakeholders, considering shareholder value and a healthy bottom line to be their lead business driver to the extent that staff numbers must be reduced to achieve profitability. Chapter 2 describes the various approaches that organisations and researchers have taken with different organisations, and Section III provides a more detailed description of typical organisations at different levels of maturity.

Examples of selection of the category of most important stakeholders[4] influenced by an organisation's culture include those shown in Table 3.3 and Box 3.4.

Table 3.3   Cultural bias in stakeholder selection

Employees or managers from these organisations	Cultural focus for selection of stakeholders
Traditional (emerging nations) Conservative government organisations	Government entities (either as a whole or as different departments or divisions of government) Elected leaders
US Corporations	Customers
Large publicly-listed corporations	Company's shareholders
Medium-sized organisations: particularly those with rapid growth in business and staff	Senior managers or the company's leadership team

---

4   This question is part of the early exercise in the *Successful Stakeholder Management* course from 2005. It is recorded as part of the team discussions within the workshop environment. The conclusions have been drawn from data collected in this exercise and subsequent discussions with workshop participants.

BOX 3.4   PATTERNS IN STAKEHOLDER IMPORTANCE FROM WORKSHOPS

I have also noted patterns emerging on how stakeholders are viewed, and who is seen to be the most important, in the stakeholder management workshops I have led since 2003. These workshops are managed through PMI® and held at regular intervals in the US and at the end of their Global Congresses. Staff or employees, team members, or end users of the outcomes of the work, who are all key stakeholders in any business change activity, are rarely mentioned in these workshops. Some outstanding examples are: the users of IT applications are the stakeholders who will be responsible for using the new tool or technique for the benefit of the organisation; end users of major constructions, such as the fans of Wembley Stadium, were not considered as the most important stakeholders during its construction or plans for operation and were unhappy with the increased cost of admission; BA staff were asked to volunteer for training in the use of the new facilities of T5, resulting in many staff not knowing what they were supposed to do when the terminal opened.

As history has shown, whether the implementation of new IT applications, the use of Wembley Stadium or the opening of T5, the oversight or neglect of these important stakeholders leads to loss of reputation and less than optimal start to operations of the new facilities. In a more general perspective, culturally significant stakeholders will be intrinsically important to the work by the very nature of the culture of that organisation. However, this cultural bias must be balanced through the use of empirical information collection methods to enable the team to engage all important and key stakeholders.

HOW TO UNDERSTAND WHO IS IMPORTANT

The results from *step 1: identify* are the starting point for *step 2: prioritise*. For complex high-profile activities, the unranked, unrefined list can be quite large.[5] With large numbers of stakeholders, the team will need to understand which of these stakeholders are more important *at this time*. Some individual managers or team members may instinctively know who is important, but others may not have the necessary experience or awareness. In long-running complex organisation activities where team membership is constantly changing, it is essential to develop a consistent approach to decisions about who actually is important at any particular time.

Step 2: prioritise in the **Stakeholder** *Circle* methodology provides a system for rating and therefore ranking stakeholders according to their relative importance to the work at a particular time. The ratings are based on three aspects:

1.   *Power:* the power an individual or group may have to permanently change or stop the project or other work.

---

5   In working with organisations using the **Stakeholder** *Circle* methodology and software for mapping and managing stakeholder relationships, the author has assisted in projects that have over 100 stakeholders (both individuals and groups) identified in the first step.

2.   *Proximity:* the degree of involvement that the individual or group has in the work of the team.

3.   *Urgency:* the importance of the work or its outcomes, whether positive or negative, to certain stakeholders (their stake), and how prepared they are to act to achieve these outcomes (stake). *Urgency* is difficult to define and rate consistently[6] and has been further divided into two sub-categories: defining the *value* of the stake to the stakeholder and then defining the level of *action* that the stakeholder is prepared to take to attain that value.

The team applies the knowledge they have gained through *step 1: identify,* discussing and agreeing on which of the rating statements, for 1–4 for *power,* and *proximity,* (where 4 is the highest rating) and 1–5 for each of the two parts of *urgency* – *value* and *action* (where 5 is highest). Table 3.4 lists the ratings for *power* and *proximity,* and Table 3.5 opposite lists the ratings for *value* and *action.*

Table 3.4   Ratings for *power* and *proximity*

Power	4. High capacity to formally instruct change: can have the work stopped. 3. Some capacity to formally instruct change: must be consulted or has to approve. 2. Significant informal capacity to cause change. 1. Relatively low levels of power: cannot generally cause much change.
Proximity	4. Directly involved in the work: team members working most of the time. 3. Routinely involved in the work: part-time team members, external suppliers and active sponsors. 2. Detached from the work but has regular contact with, or input to, the work processes. 1. Relatively remote from the work: does not have direct involvement with processes: clients and most senior managers.

WHY CHOOSE THESE PRIORITISATION ATTRIBUTES?

The three attributes of *power, proximity and urgency* are the essential elements for understanding which stakeholders are more important than others at any specific time over the total timeframe of the project or other organisational work. The work of researchers (Savage, Nix, Whitehead and Blair 1991;

---

6   During the 12 months research in development of this methodology, it became evident that the concept of *urgency* was too multi-dimensional for consistency. Once the concept was developed in two parts – *value* and *action* – it was possible to apply the new ratings consistently.

Table 3.5   Ratings for *urgency*

Ratings for urgency		
Value: How much stake does the person have in the work or its outcomes?	5.	Very high: has great personal stake in the work's outcome (success/cancellation).
	4.	High: sees work's outcome as being important (benefit or threat) to self or organisation.
	3.	Medium: has some direct stake in the outcome of the work.
	2.	Low: is aware of work and has an indirect stake in work's outcome.
	1.	Very low: has very limited or no stake in work's outcome.
Action: A measure of the likelihood that the stakeholder will take action, positive or negative, to influence the work or its outcomes	5.	Very high: self-activated, will go to almost any length to influence the work.
	4.	High: is likely to make a significant effort to influence the work.
	3.	Medium: may be prepared to make an effort to influence the work.
	2.	Low: has the potential to attempt to influence the work.
	1.	Very low: is unlikely to attempt to influence the work.

Mitchell, Agle and Wood 1997) has been described in Chapter 2. The focus of the former is on stakeholder relationships that are unique for each issue and situation. The latter have defined stakeholder importance in the context of *power, legitimacy* (relationship with the firm) and *urgency* (of the claim on the firm). Both of these seminal works influenced the selection of the ratings for this methodology.

Power

Power has been defined as the 'ability to get things done' (Lovell 1993; Pinto 1998). The nature of power and influence, the sources of this power and the way in which it is used to contribute to or manipulate cooperative relationships underpin all relationships whether personal, work related or organisational. Power can be understood as a necessary part of the structure of relationships, and as neither good nor bad. Power exists in organisations through hierarchical structures; the exercise of power is a political process, and all relationships are power relationships (Stacey 2001).

The definition of *power* used in *step 2: prioritise* describes the relative power to 'kill' or 'save' the work or activity, or cause permanent change. In this methodology it is not necessary to identify the type of power that a stakeholder wields. It is essential only to understand the extent to which the stakeholder has power over the continuation of the work itself, the extent to which he or she must be consulted, or at the lowest level, that he or she has no power at all.

Proximity

The rating *proximity* provides a second way of identifying how a stakeholder may influence the work or its outcomes. Its contribution is the acknowledgement of the importance of regular, close and often face-to-face relationships in influencing the outcomes of the work. The immediacy of this relationship contributes to trust between members of the team, and more effective work relationships as the team members understand the strengths and weaknesses of those they work with on a regular basis (Granovetter 1973). An individual's ability to access independently all other members of the team (Rowley 1997), develops a stronger team culture, and enhances the team's ability to achieve group goals. Groups work best when they have met each other (face-to-face) at least once; and that they work even more effectively if co-located (McGrath 1984).[7]

Urgency

Urgency is based on the concept described in (Mitchell, Agle et al. 1997) whose theory described two conditions that may contribute to the notion of urgency:

1. Time sensitivity: work that must be completed in a fixed time, such as a facility for the Olympic Games.

2. Criticality: an individual or group feels strongly enough about an issue to act, such as environmental or heritage protection activists.

In the **Stakeholder** *Circle, urgency* is rated through analysis of two sub-categories: the *value* that a stakeholder places on an outcome of the work, and the *action* that he or she is prepared to take as a consequence of this value or stake. The inclusion of *urgency* in the prioritisation ratings balances the potential distortion of an organisational culture that identifies the stakeholder with a high level of hierarchical power as most important. If *power* and *proximity* are the only measures, stakeholders such as the lone powerless voice who can cause significant damage to successful outcomes if ignored, will not be acknowledged.

---

7   This research, conducted in the 1980s may soon be superseded by research into Generation Y's communication preferences for online forms and text messaging. The **Stakeholder** *Circle* simply defines *proximity* by involvement in the work of the teams.

The prioritisation process

The team rates the list of stakeholders from *step 1: identify* against the statements for *power, proximity, value* and *action,* agreeing on the rating and recording it.

The index number

The stakeholder's index number is calculated from the four sets of ratings developed by the team. Calculations are inbuilt in the **Stakeholder** Circle software or the Excel worksheet. For paper-based use of the methodology, the arithmetic addition of all four ratings will be sufficient. This emphasis on ratings for *urgency* will ensure visibility of stakeholders who may not be considered as important to the project or the work within the prevailing organisational culture (Mitchell, Agle et al. 1997; Walker, Bourne et al. 2008).[8] After the index number is calculated, the list can be sorted: the stakeholder with the highest index number is rated as the most important, the second highest next most important and so on. This ranked stakeholder list must now be tested for reality against the knowledge and experience of the team and perhaps other senior managers within the organisation. After review and any necessary amendments the ranked list of stakeholders will provide valuable information to the team, and may also be useful in many other ways. The effectiveness of revealing who the key stakeholders are will be discussed in Chapter 4.

Conclusion

This chapter described the first two steps to enable teams to develop a better understanding of their stakeholder community. In a large organisation, or a highly political one, or if the work is high-profile, a large number of stakeholders will be identified. Prioritisation is part of the filtering process that reduces the work-load of the team, and provides the means to understand who is important and a focus for gathering information about these important stakeholders. The prioritisation process is not just about applying the numbers from the ratings; it also provides the focus for essential discussion about this community. The results of this discussion are identification of its unique characteristics, and direction on how to manage the essential stakeholder relationships. The rating

---

8   By weighting *urgency* more highly than *power* or *proximity* the methodology helps team members identify less obvious, or less outspoken, stakeholders thus ensuring that 'surprises' are minimised. Generally, those stakeholders with *power* in the stakeholder community will be relatively easy to identify, but those with high levels of *urgency* may not be.

structure based on standard consistent statements provides a robust framework for analysis and discussion about members of the community who 'matter', and recognising that all stakeholders are not the same and should not all be treated the same.

In this chapter the *Stakeholder Circle* was described as a specific construct based on providing a structure to support teams in understanding which stakeholders are important and providing the means to develop and maintain robust relationships with them. The next chapter describes the theory and history of stakeholder mapping and defines ways to analyse and present this information for best effect.

Mapping Stakeholders

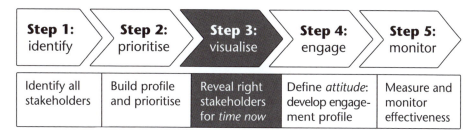

Step 1: identify	Step 2: prioritise	Step 3: visualise	Step 4: engage	Step 5: monitor
Identify all stakeholders	Build profile and prioritise	Reveal right stakeholders for *time now*	Define *attitude*: develop engage-ment profile	Measure and monitor effectiveness

Figure 4.1   Chapter 4 focus

Chapter 3 described the first two *steps* of the **Stakeholder** *Circle* methodology, *step 1: identify* and *step 2: prioritise*. The results of these *steps* will enable teams to develop a better understanding of the unique characteristics of their stakeholder community and the relationships within it. The standard rating structure provides a robust framework for analysis and discussion about members of the community who matter. The rating structure also reinforces the concept that all stakeholders are not the same and should not all be treated in the same way. This chapter describes the theory and history of stakeholder mapping and defines ways to analyse and present stakeholder information to enhance understanding – *step 3: visualise*. It is organised as follows: the first section provides a brief overview of the importance of unambiguous and clear presentation of complex data; the second section traces the history of the idea of using diagrams to convey information. This is followed by a description of the multiple methods and techniques that have been, and are, in use for representing stakeholder concepts and communities. The final section describes the tools that support visualisation in the **Stakeholder** *Circle* methodology.

Presentation of complex data

The objective of every stakeholder mapping process is to:

- develop a useful list of stakeholders;

- assess some of their key characteristics;

- present the list in a way that assists the team's implementation of planned stakeholder relationship management initiatives.

The key elements of an effective mapping process are to:

- reduce subjectivity as much as possible;

- make the assessment process transparent;

- make the complex data collected about the stakeholders easy to understand;

- provide a sound basis for analysis and discussion.

Presenting complex data effectively will be directly useful to two important stakeholder groups:

- management within the organisation;

- the team responsible for delivery the outcomes of the activity.

MANAGEMENT

When presenting complex data it is important to consider ways to help other managers appreciate and understand the information being presented. This understanding is a vital first step in the process that allows them to apply their experience effectively and contribute to wise decision-making. Presentation of complex information in several complementary forms, such as graphical or pictorial views supported by tabulations and/or sorted lists will enhance this process.

THE TEAM

Team members who have participated in the development of data describing their stakeholder community can benefit from the effective use of charts and graphics in two ways:

1. Categorising the data gathered about the activity's stakeholders through *steps 1 and 2* allows the team to manage otherwise

unwieldy data and possibly gain valuable insights about patterns of stakeholder coalitions or behaviour.

2. The assessment team needs to help other team members and managers to absorb or make sense of the data. Presenting data in graphical or pictorial form will help others map connections more readily.

The brain processes ideas fastest visually (Rock 2006: 90). Studies have also shown that individuals learn best and retain information longer when offered the data in more than one mode. For example, learning is enhanced through absorbing new information by the combined processes of listening and seeing, and even better by listening, seeing and doing (Glasser 1998). Therefore, the complex data collected about stakeholders will be most easily understood by others when presented in several complementary forms, such as the appropriate combination of:

- graphical or pictorial views;

- tables and/or sorted lists;

- written explanation;

- discussion.

The History of Stakeholder Mapping

Today, most branches of science, management and the general media routinely use charts, graphs and pictures to communicate and simplify complex representation of ideas. However, the practice of using diagrams to help understand complex, multi-dimensional data is relatively new. The first major published work using images to convey complex information was published in 1786 (Playfair 1801), with graphical forms including the pie chart, line graph and the bar chart (histogram), used as an aid to analysis and memory (Wainer and Spence 2005).

Scientific data had been available as numerical tables for at least a century before Playfair published his *Atlas* (Playfair 1801). However, many of the leading thinkers of that era opposed the use of diagrams on philosophical grounds.

Robert Hooke,[1] who used illustrations extensively, did so with misgivings, expressing concern about an illustration's potential for misrepresentation of the data (Wainer and Spence 2005). The general use of illustrations continued to be rejected by most scientists through to the middle of the nineteenth century, due to concerns about misrepresenting and distorting information. Even in the twenty-first century some leading academics express concern about the use of 'corrupt manipulations and rhetorical ploys', describing making a presentation as 'a moral act as well as an intellectual activity' (Tufte 2006: intro). Despite these concerns it is now common practice to support written descriptions with graphics or tabulated data to augment the more detailed information of the written word.

STAKEHOLDER REPRESENTATIONS

When considering the communication of complex multi-dimensional information about stakeholders, the challenge is to present the information in a way that illuminates the issues and creates understanding without distorting the message. Essentially three different views of stakeholder have been attempted:

- classes of stakeholder in relation to the organisation (Figure 4.2);

- typology of stakeholders and the interrelationship between types (Figure 4.3);

- specific stakeholders plotted against various parameters (Figures 4.4 to 4.11).

CLASSES OF STAKEHOLDER

This style of representation essentially looks at the proximity of stakeholders to the activity in a series of expanding circles. Each circle may represent an entire type of stakeholder, or different types of stakeholder. Stakeholders at approximately the same distance from the activity can be defined by annotations within the diagram. Figure 4.2 shows this type of representation.

This style of diagram is useful for displaying an overview of which *stakeholder class* is likely to be most influential but it can only effectively deal with a single data dimension such as *proximity*, or *influence*.

---

1   He developed Hooke's Law on the properties of elasticity of loads on extended springs, also credited with developing the concept of 'cell' as the basic unit of life: retrieved from Wikipedia, January, 2009.

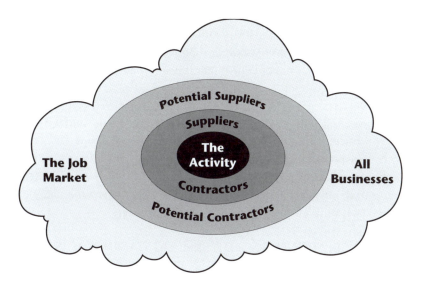

Figure 4.2   Stakeholder classes

STAKEHOLDER TYPES AND RELATIONSHIPS

This type of chart effectively develops a list of *stakeholder types* and will frequently show their relationships with each other as well as to/from the activity. Figure 4.3 shows the major stakeholders impacting an activity and some of the key interrelationships. In this representation, the media can influence

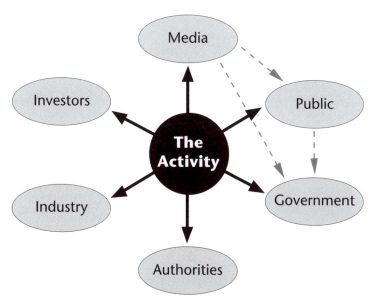

Figure 4.3   Stakeholder typology

the government both directly and through influencing the public. This type of diagram can display more complex data by using different line styles and shapes. It is capable of displaying relationships amongst the stakeholder types.

The representations of stakeholders shown in Figures 4.2 and 4.3 have been used by commentators and researchers in a variety of styles and layouts to demonstrate aspects of the complex interrelationship between an activity and its stakeholders. However, while being useful for clarifying concepts and ideas pertaining to the overall subject of stakeholder relationship management, the format makes it difficult to map individual stakeholders.

PRESENTING RELATIONSHIPS WITH SPECIFIC STAKEHOLDERS

The third type of representation is significant to supporting the work of stakeholder relationship management within the *Stakeholder Circle* methodology. It is the foundation for information to support the team in formulating strategies and making decisions to best focus their limited resources. The information assists the team to be aware of stakeholders who:

- need further levels of effort beyond current practice;

- should only receive routine attention, as defined in current processes and practices.

Designing visual aids that convey useful information about stakeholders is not straightforward. A two-dimensional, flat sheet of paper cannot easily present the multi-faceted relationship likely to exist between the team and their stakeholders. Some of the dimensions that may need to be considered include:

- attitude (will the person help or hinder the work?);

- hierarchy (where is the person in the organisation's structure compared to the activity manager: higher/lower, internal/external, colleague or competitor?);

- influence (how well connected is the person?);

- interest (does the person have an active interest, passive interest or no interest at all?);

- legitimacy (does the person have some level of 'right' to be consulted?);

- power (what is the person's ability to instruct or cause change?);

- proximity (how involved is the person in the work?);

- receptiveness (how easy is it to communicate with this person?);

- supportiveness (does the person support or oppose the work?);

- urgency (does the person have time issues or do they perceive the work as important to them?).

This list is far from exhaustive but serves to demonstrate the challenges of deciding which stakeholders matter, and the nature of the relationship between each stakeholder (individual or group) and the team.

Stakeholder Identification Tools

A number of schemas have been developed to describe the relationships between specific stakeholders and the activity. These include:

- influence map (Figure 4.4);

- project environment map (Figure 4.5);

- various versions of the 'two by two' matrix (Figure 4.6);

- engagement profile matrix from the *Stakeholder Circle* methodology (Figure 4.9).

An additional depiction typology has been developed to overcome the tyranny of the two-dimensional representation. Examples are:

- the three-dimensional grid: the stakeholder cube (Figure 4.7);

- the *Stakeholder Circle* community representation developed by the *Stakeholder Circle* database: the Stakeholder Information Management System (SIMS) (Figure 4.8).

THE INFLUENCE MAP

The influence map was designed for use in policy development in the 1980s to depict the influence of selected stakeholders. It uses a triangular construct with the activity at its apex. It provides two dimensions of data about stakeholders:

1. The nearer to the apex the position of the stakeholder symbol, the greater the influence of that stakeholder.

2. The size of the circle represents the significance of the stakeholder.

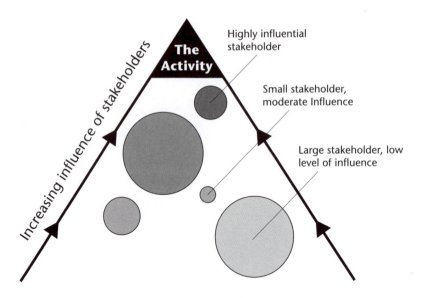

Figure 4.4   The stakeholder influence map

THE ENVIRONMENT MAP

The environmental map supports a more complex view of the overall environment of the activity and includes key stakeholders in an overall environment scan, with an additional consideration of risk. This tool was developed for use on World Bank projects (Youker 1992).

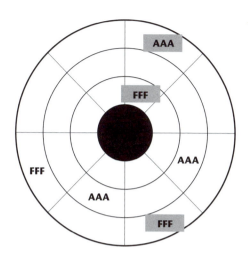

Concentric Circles
Proximity – local/regional/national

Sectors
Type or class of exposure – e.g.,:
technological, political, financial

Factors and Actors
Factors = sources of risk (FFF)
Actors = stakeholders (AAA)
Boxes = important factors or
actors

Factors and Actors are written into
the chart in the appropriate
location and the important ones
highlighted

Figure 4.5   The project environment map

In effect, both schema (Figures 4.4 and 4.5) represent a stakeholder mapping methodology and a visualisation tool. The work of creating the diagram helps those involved to build a deeper appreciation of their stakeholder community.

STANDARD 2X2 MATRIX

Probably the most common tool used to represent stakeholders is the 2x2 matrix. The matrix represents two dimensions of stakeholder attributes, with sometimes a third or fourth dimension shown by the colour and/or sise of the symbol representing the individual stakeholders. This is summarised in Figure 4.6.

Some of the commonly used stakeholder attributes include:

- power (low, medium or high);

- support (negative, neutral or positive);

- influence (low or high);

- interest (low or high);

- attitude (obstructive or supportive).

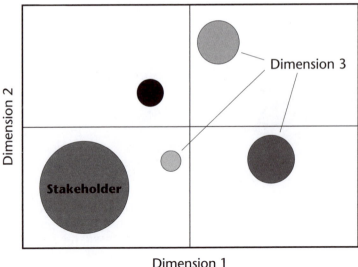

Figure 4.6   A generic 2x2 matrix

Probably the most common combination is the power/influence matrix with colours (green/amber/red) indicating support or opposition for the activity.

THREE-DIMENSIONAL STAKEHOLDER GRID

The three-dimensional stakeholder cube is a more sophisticated development of this style of chart. The methodology supports the mapping of stakeholders':

- interest (active or passive);

- power (influential or insignificant);

- attitude (backer or blocker).

The theory supporting the grid mapping format includes the development of eight typologies with suggestions on the optimum approach to managing the stakeholder (Murray-Webster and Simon 2008).[2] However, the nature of the chart makes it difficult to draw specific stakeholders in the grid, or show any relationships between stakeholders and the activity.

---

2   For more information see www.lucidusconsulting.com

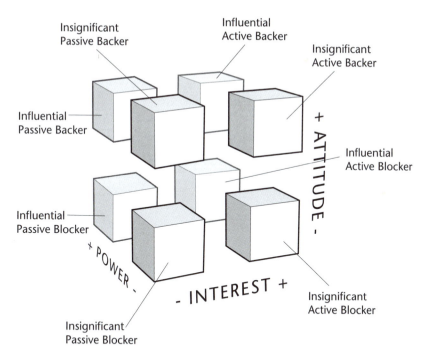

Figure 4.7   Stakeholder cube

ENGAGEMENT PROFILE

The *Stakeholder Circle* methodology uses two diagrams to help understand relationships with an activity's stakeholders. The primary diagram is the *Stakeholder Circle* after which the methodology is named. This chart focuses on highlighting the stakeholders that matter and defining which stakeholders are important at this time in the activity's life cycle. It will be described in detail later in this chapter. The engagement profile matrix is the second schema. It is used to assess the current and desirable *attitude* of each stakeholder.[3] Its purpose is to support the team's planning for proactive communication with the stakeholders whose engagement profile is shown as needing additional effort to:

- cause a positive change in the stakeholder's *attitude*; or

- ensure the stakeholder maintains critical support for the activity.

---

3   The current and target *attitude* are then displayed as the engagement profile.

The *Stakeholder Circle* was explicitly designed to highlight 'who matters'. Consequently, the data gathered as part of *step 1: identify* and *step 2: prioritise* are neutral in regard to the support or opposition of any particular stakeholder to the activity. The *Stakeholder Circle* assessment seeks to balance:

- The significance of a stakeholder who is important to the activity because they provide funding and support; with

- The significance of a key stakeholder strongly opposed to the activity who is expressing that opposition through actions such as:

  - organising protests;

  - lobbying government ministers.

The engagement profile matrix is different; it displays the *attitude* of stakeholders in terms of their *support* for the activity and their willingness to receive messages about the activity (*receptiveness)* compared with the project team's desired target *attitude* for the stakeholder – this is their *engagement profile*. It may be positive or negative. Figure 4.8 shows the engagement profiles for three different stakeholders. The chart is a 5x5 matrix, the 'X' symbols indicating the current assessed *attitude* of the stakeholder and the 'O' symbol the desired *attitude* to optimise the success of the activity.

Comparing engagement profiles from different stakeholders within the current stakeholder community helps the team to focus their communication efforts by:

- understanding the difference (the gap) between the existing and target *attitude* for the stakeholder;

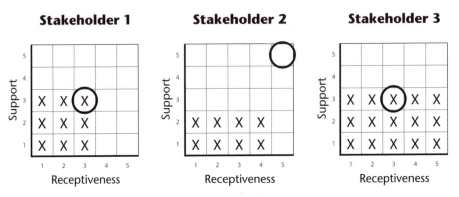

Figure 4.8   Example of engagement profile matrix

- using this information to determine what course of action (or communication) is realistically achievable; and

- assessing the level of effort necessary to close the gap, based on the relative importance of these stakeholders;

- planning and implementing the appropriate communication strategy.

Chapters 5 and 6 focus on the engagement process and discuss the types of communication potentially needed to influence the *attitude* of a stakeholder based on the information in the engagement profile. The key benefits of a simple representation such as the engagement profile are to:

- assist individual team members absorb, interpret and understand the data;

- act as a focus point for team discussion;

- provide a visual record of changes to each stakeholder's *attitude* over time;

- provide a valuable reference to decisions made about managing specific relationships;

- provide support to complementary records such as:

  - formal minutes or other records of meetings;

  - action lists;

  - updates to communication plans and schedules.

Figure 4.8 represents a snapshot of complex data about three stakeholder relationships. A series of these snapshots provides additional value through allowing comparisons of changes noted in the content of each snapshot, showing evidence that the relationship management strategies have been:

- successful – the results indicate that the action has had the intended outcome;

- unsuccessful – the action has not achieved the intended outcome, perhaps indicating that the opposite of the intended outcome was actually attained;

- unchanged – there has been no change, requiring further investigation and analysis.[4]

THE STAKEHOLDER CIRCLE

The *Stakeholder Circle* shows a multi-dimensional map of the activity's stakeholder community, produced from data gathered during *steps 1 and 2* of the *Stakeholder Circle* methodology. Key elements of the *Stakeholder Circle* are:

- Concentric circles indicate distance of stakeholders from the work of the activity or project.

- The size of the block represented by its relative length on the outer circumference indicates the scale and scope of influence of the stakeholder.

- The radial depth of the segment indicates the stakeholder's degree of power.

- Colours indicate the stakeholder's *direction of influence*[5] relative to the activity:

  - Orange indicates an *upwards* direction – these stakeholders are senior managers within the performing organisation that are necessary for ongoing organisational commitment to the activity.

  - Green indicates a *downwards* direction – these stakeholders are typically members of the project team or suppliers of services needed by the activity.

  - Purple indicates a *sidewards* direction – peers of the activity manager either as collaborators or competitors.

---

4   Examples of these situations are described in Chapter 6.
5   Chapter 3 describes the *directions of influence* in detail.

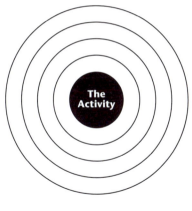

The **Stakeholder** Circle represents the work of the activity surrounded by its stakeholder community.

The activity leader or project manager represents the work, and all dimensions of the stakeholder analysis are relative to this person; e.g., *downwards* represents the team members working for the leader.

Four concentric circles represent the *proximity* of the stakeholders to the work and their *power*. The closer a stakeholder is to the work, the nearer it will be drawn to the centre of the circle.

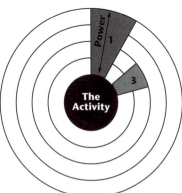

Stakeholders are represented by segments of the circle.

The *power* of the stakeholder is represented by the radial depth of the segment.

Stakeholder 1 has a *power* of 4 and can 'kill' the project; it 'cuts the circle'. This person is a key stakeholder.

Stakeholder 3 has a *power* rating of 2, a significant informal capacity to cause change. This stakeholder is also very close to the work, possibly a team member.

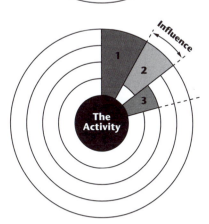

The importance of each stakeholder and their degree of influence is indicated by the relative size of each segment measured on the outer circumference of the circle. The larger the segment, the more influential the stakeholder.

The most important stakeholder (with the highest level of influence) is plotted at position 1, starting at 12:00 o'clock, the second most important is next, through to the 15th most important.*

Finally, colours and shadings indicate the direction of influence of the stakeholder and whether the stakeholder is internal or external to the organisation.

*Note: The design constraint in the **Stakeholder** Circle to plot the top 15 stakeholders does not mean these are the only important stakeholders or that every activity should always manage all 15. The number of important stakeholders that need active management is entirely dependent on the nature of the activity. The choice of 15 stakeholders for the **Stakeholder** Circle display was based on empirical observation of 'who mattered' during the development of the tool.

Figure 4.9   **Reading the *Stakeholder Circle***

- Blue indicates *outwards* – these stakeholders represent those outside the activity such as end users, government, the public and shareholders.

- Colour intensity differentiates stakeholders *internal* to the organisation (dark hues and patterns) and light hues and patterns for those *external* to the organisation.

The most important stakeholder for the Asset Management Project shown in Figure 4.10 has been assessed as the sponsor: this stakeholder appears at the 12 o'clock position. The second most important is the project team, and the Chief Executive Officer (CEO) is shown as the third most important stakeholder.

REFLECTION OF THE CULTURE OF THE STAKEHOLDER COMMUNITY

The *Stakeholder Circle* mapping of the stakeholder community will be different for each activity or project and for each phase of the work, reflecting the unique stakeholder community that exists at that particular point in time. Each visualisation of an activity's stakeholder community should be expected to be different, but should also show some features that will be common to an organisation or an activity type. Where an organisation undertakes similar activities on a regular basis, it is highly likely a normal pattern[6] of stakeholders will emerge. When a normal stakeholder community has been established as a baseline, a significant deviation may indicate a risk or a problem: this should be the trigger for additional analysis and investigation.

Some changes within any stakeholder community are to be expected. For example, the degree of importance attached to the end users of a new airport terminal may be relatively low during the early phases of the work where the key focus is on obtaining design approvals and funding. However, as the opening day approaches, the expectations and actual experiences of both airline staff and passengers (the end users) will become increasingly important and this should correspond to a higher ranking in the *Stakeholder Circle*. This type of change can be observed in the tool and with thought, a logical explanation is apparent. In this circumstance, the value of the chart is in ensuring the right degree of focus is attached to the stakeholder relationship management effort for important stakeholders.

---

6   A normal pattern in this context is one that shows what a well-functioning stakeholder community will look like in this culture.

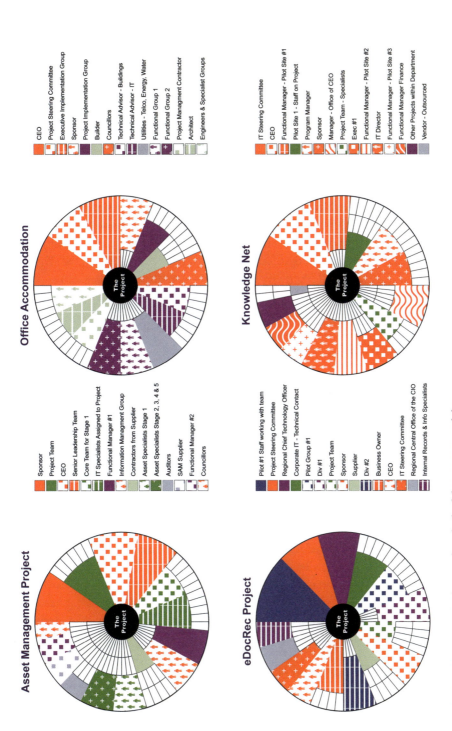

Office Accommodation

CEO
Project Steering Committee
Executive Implementation Group
Sponsor
Project Implementation Group
Builder
Councillors
Technical Advisor - Buildings
Technical Advisor - IT
Utilities - Telco, Energy, Water
Functional Group 1
Functional Group 2
Project Management Contractor
Architect
Engineers & Specialist Groups

Sponsor
Project Team
CEO
Senior Leadership Team
Core Team for Stage 1
IT Specialists Assigned to Project
Functional Manager #1
Information Managment Group
Contractors from Supplier
Asset Specialists Stage 1
Asset Specialists Stage 2, 3, 4 & 5
Auditors
SAM Supplier
Functional Manager #2
Councillors

Asset Management Project

Knowledge Net

IT Steering Committee
CEO
Functional Manager - Pilot Site #1
Pilot Site 1 - Staff on Project
Program Manager
Sponsor
Manager - Office of CEO
Project Team - Specialists
Exec #1
Functional Manager - Pilot Site #2
IT Director
Functional Manager - Pilot Site #3
Functional Manager Finance
Other Projects within Department
Vendor - Outsourced

Pilot #1 Staff working with team
Project Steering Committee
Regional Chief Technology Officer
Corporate IT - Technical Contact
Pilot Group #1
Div #1
Project Team
Sponsor
Supplier
Div #2
Business Owner
CEO
IT Steering Committee
Regional Central Office of the CIO
Internal Records & Info Specialists

eDocRec Project

Figure 4.10   Representations of stakeholder communities

When the tool highlights an unexpected change, more significant action is required. The first question should be 'What has caused the anomaly?' From the results of the investigation, a formal issue may need to be raised, a remedy may need to be introduced or risk mitigation activities may be required. The interpretation of a stakeholder community and the relationships within it can provide an early warning indicator of tensions arising from other problems within the community.

COMMON CHARACTERISTICS OF A STAKEHOLDER COMMUNITY

Data has been collected through the process of building representations of the stakeholder communities in many organisations, resulting in the emergence of some common characteristics of stakeholder communities. These characteristics seem to be independent of organisational, national or industry culture. The 15 most important stakeholders in any community usually comprise:

- the CEO, the sponsor and steering committees;

- the team;

- *outwards* stakeholders, who represent at least 30 per cent, except for activities focused on internal deliverables;

- relatively small numbers of *downwards* and *sidewards* stakeholders.

FOUR DIFFERENT STAKEHOLDER COMMUNITIES

Figure 4.10 demonstrates how four stakeholder communities can be depicted and how these representations can provide information to trigger further investigation. Four stakeholder communities are represented:

- the Asset Management IT implementation;

- Office Accommodation update and consequent change management activity;

- the KnowledgeNet programme consisting of:

  - hardware acquisition;

- – process re-engineering;

- – software development;

- – training and awareness.

- • eDocRec: electronic documents and records management implementation programme consisting of:

  - – pilot implementation and assessment;

  - – process re-engineering;

  - – software customisation;

  - – implementation and change management;

  - – continuous training and organisational awareness;

  - – hardware acquisition.

The first two stakeholder communities exhibit no extraordinary characteristics. There is a reasonable mixture of stakeholders both in terms of *internal* and *external* to the organisation and *direction of influence*. On the other hand, the KnowledgeNet programme highlights a systemic problem in the organisation's structure. Almost the whole of the team's time is directed to dealing with requests for ad hoc reports and unscheduled attendance at management meetings, with resulting damage to efforts to achieve scheduled deliverables. The *Stakeholder Circle* does not show this level of detail; it only indicates that there is a high proportion of *upwards* stakeholders assessed as being important to the success of the programme. The predominance of influence of these senior stakeholders acted as a trigger for investigation, as well as visual support for the difficult situation the team found itself in, but could not express. This *Stakeholder Circle* was used as evidence to explain the schedule slip and the basis for the team's reports of unscheduled and ad hoc reporting requirements. A remedy was found: a programme manager appointed to deal with *upwards* communications; the team was then able to focus on the work of delivering the programme outcomes.

The *Stakeholder Circle* for the eDocRec programme highlighted a completely different issue. When the chart was created, the most important stakeholder, by a significant margin, was deemed to be staff in one of the pilot sites working with the implementation team. These stakeholders were rated as *outwards* rather than *downwards* (part of the team) or *sidewards* (peers of the implementation team members). This unexpected result triggered an investigation into the relationships in that particular community. Alerted to the problem that was revealed, the organisation's management took appropriate steps to remedy the situation, and the programme continued without any further concern.

Even in the first two relatively normal programmes, the *Stakeholder Circles* provided insights into the culture of the organisation and the team. For example, the Asset Management implementation programme was potentially a high-risk activity. It involved migrating data from a range of well- established, stand-alone reporting systems into an integrated database. To avoid problems with the existing system owners, the manager integrated the managers of each section into her team in an inclusive and supportive way. This in part reflected the character of the (experienced) manager and in part the ethos of the organisation. The effect is highlighted in the *Stakeholder* Circle by the number of green segments.

The Office Accommodation update programme involved temporarily moving staff from their existing building while it was being renovated and then relocating them back into the finished facility. The highly political nature of this activity can be seen in the number of peers of the team, shown in the representation of the stakeholder community. These are other managers impacted by the activity but not under the direct control of its manager. The situation called for a competent negotiator who could build strong relationships with people; this was reinforced by the way in which the important stakeholders of this activity were presented in the *Stakeholder* Circle.

Stakeholder Circle supporting tools

Implementing the *Stakeholder* Circle methodology is not dependent on any software tool. It is possible to apply the methodology effectively using manual records and basic reporting systems. Choosing an appropriate tool will depend on a combination of:

- the maturity of the organisation;

- the complexity of the activity being analysed;

- the objective of the analysis.

The analysis and reporting requirements of a multi billion dollar project extending over several years are quite different from the requirements of a small pre-tender stakeholder analysis focused on understanding the potential client and the competitive environment.

The three tools discussed below have been specifically developed to support the **Stakeholder** *Circle* methodology at different levels of sophistication, but are not essential for its use. The three tools are:

1. Stakeholder-on-a-page™ (SOAP);

2. Stakeholder WorkSheet (SWS);

3. Stakeholder Information Management System (SIMS).

SOAP

The *stakeholder-on-a-page* is a preformatted MS Word template designed to record stakeholder information and allow three updates of assessments of an activity's stakeholder community (see Figure 4.11). The advantages of this tool are:

- ease of use:

  - information is written onto the sheet (or entered on screen) and is readily available for review and assessment.

  - it is supported by simple technology which is easy to use.

  - it allows the assessment team to focus on understanding and managing relationships with its stakeholders, rather than the intricacies of the technology.

- ability to store the data and measure trends:

  - on the printed SOAP template as a permanent record; or

  - electronically as a MS Word document.

Stakeholder *Management Pty Ltd*

stakeholder-on-a-page

Stakeholder Name _____

Directions of Influence: **U__D__O__S__ and I__E__**

Requires from the work: _____

Importance to the work: _____

Stake	
I __	R __
O __	N __
I __	C __

Prioritise the Stakeholder

Assessment	Power Rate 1 - 4	Proximity Rate 1 - 4	Value Rate 1 - 5	Action Rate 1 - 5	Index # / Priority #

Build Engagement Profile (see note)

First assessment — Support (1–5) vs Receptiveness (1–5)

Next assessment — Support (1–5) vs Receptiveness (1–5)

Next assessment — Support (1–5) vs Receptiveness (1–5)

Use **X** when assessing the <u>current</u> engagement profile of each stakeholder and **O** to indicate the <u>optimal</u> engagement profile

*Influence on?*_____ *Influenced by?*_____

Communication Plan

Message	Messenger	Format (W/O F/I)	Frequency	Assessment date	Comments

Relationship Manager: owns the relationship _____

Figure 4.11   SOAP template

The key disadvantage of SOAP is that it is dependent on manual processes, hence there is a lack of:

- automatic calculation aids: the calculation of each stakeholder's index value is manual;

- sorting capabilities: sorting into priority order is also a manual process.

This dependence on manual processes limits the usefulness of the tool to small-scale activities that involve a relatively small number of stakeholders. Figure 4.9 shows the front page of the SOAP template. The back page (not shown here) is used as a temporary placeholder for issues that have arisen during communication with stakeholders.

SWS

The *Stakeholder WorkSheet* (SWS) is designed for the analysis of relatively large groups of stakeholders. Built in Excel, the tool facilitates the rapid calculation and analysis of data, followed by the sorting and display of information. Its graphical displays are effective but limited by the inability of the worksheet to store data for comparison. This tool is ideal for use in rapidly changing situations such as:

- bidding for a major long term contract to operate a facility; or

- analysis of the stakeholder issues around a one-off event such as an Olympic Torch relay.

Within SWS information is built progressively. Data from *step 1: identify* is shown in Figure 4.12, *step 2: prioritise* is shown in Figure 4.13. *Step 2* prioritises the stakeholders. Facilities are provided to sort information by either the line number or priority. Visualisation is limited to lists and simple representations.

Step 3: visualise representation of the stakeholder community is limited to sorted lists and simple representations. The spreadsheet will identify and list the top 15 most important stakeholders in a separate report. *Step 4: engage* data is shown in Figure 4.15, in comparison to the same data displayed in the SOAP template (Figure 4.9).

Step 5: monitor cannot be shown in a single spreadsheet, although it would be possible to keep copies of the file dated at each reassessment, and make the comparisons between engagement profiles at each review.

Stakeholder Identification

- SAM Project -

Line #	Name	Direction	Role	Significance to Project	Requires from Project	Issues & Comments	Priority
1	Councillors		Represent residents				1
2	Sponsor	U	Sponsor: Project Team reports to CEO. Holds budget for SAM	Represents project to Councillors and Senior Management	Successful delivery of SAM part of KRA - delivery to stakeholder satisfaction according to scope and quality requirements on schedule		
3	General Management Team (GMT)	U	High level governance 'constitution of Sam Steering C'tee decision to come from GMT	High level governance 'constitution of Sam Steering C'tee decision to come form GMT	Successful delivery of SAM		
4	CEO	U	Responsible to Councillors	Represents project to Councillors and Senior Management	Successful delivery of SAM part of KRA - delivery to stakeholder satisfaction according to scope and quality requirements on budget on schedule		

Figure 4.12 *Step 1 data displayed in SWS*

Line #	Name	Direction	Role	Significance to Project	Requires from Project	Power	Prox.	Urg	Index	Notes	Priority
2	Sponsor	U	Sponsor: Project Team reports to CEO. Holds budget for SAM	Represents project to Councillors and Senior Management	Successful delivery of SAM part of KRA - delivery to stakeholder satisfaction according to scope and quality requirements on budget on schedule	4	2	3	35.0481		1
4	CEO	U	Responsible to Councillors	Represents project to Councillors and Senior Management	Successful delivery of SAM part of KRA - delivery to stakeholder satisfaction according to scope and quality requirements on budget on schedule	4	1	3	34.0451		2
28	Kathy and Kevin and Keith	D	Project Team	Drivers of project delivery and achievement of SAM benefits	Commitment to ensure quality, 'buy-in' from stakeholders and eventually operationalisation of SAM	3	4	3	34.0441		3

Figure 4.13 *Step 2 data displayed in SWS*

Line #	Name	Dir	Role	Significance to Project	Requires from Project	Priority	Recept-iveness	Support	Messages	Method(s)	Team Member(s)	Frequency	Notes
2	Sponsor	U	Sponsor: Project Team reports to CEO. Holds budget for SAM	Represents project to Councillors and Senior Management	Successful delivery of SAM part of KRA - delivery to stakeholder satisfaction according to scope and quality requirements on budget on schedule	1	5	4	Status Finance	I + F, W + O	KD	W	Successful delivery of SAM part of KPI. SAM CEO 'vision'
4	CEO	U	Represents project to Councillors and Senior Management	Represents project to Councillors and Senior Management	Successful delivery of SAM part of KRA - delivery to stakeholder satisfaction according to scope and quality requirements on budget on schedule	2	5	4	Exec O/View	I + F, W + O	DY	M	Successful delivery of SAM part of KPI
28	Kathy and Kevin and Keith	D	Project Team	Drivers of project delivery and achievement of SAM benefits	Commitment to ensure quality, 'buy-in' from stakeholders and eventually operationalisation of SAM	3	5	5	Weekly	O, I	KD	ad hoc	Personal satisfaction professional development

Figure 4.15 *Step 4 data displayed in SWS*

Stakeholder Circle Analysis
- SAM Project -

#	Name	Index	Power	Prox	Direction
1	Sponsor	35.0481	4	2	U
2	CEO	34.0451	4	1	U
3	Kathy and Kevin and Keith	34.0441	3	4	D
4	General Management Team (GMT)	27.0444	4	1	U
5	Core team for Stage 1 (buildings + IT infrastructure)	26.0404	3	3	D
6	IT specialists assigned to project	26.0404	3	3	D
7	SME Manager	25.0374	3	2	S
8	Auditors	25.0151	1	1	O
9	IM Group	24.0344	3	1	U
10	Contractors from successful tenderer	23.0304	2	3	D
11	Asset Specialists (Stage 1)	22.0274	2	2	D
12	Asset Specialists (Stage 2,3,4,5)	22.0274	2	2	D
13	Finance Manager	18.0144	1	1	U
14	CFO	18.0144	1	1	U
15	Steering Group	18.0144	1	1	S

Clear Top 15   Set Top 15

Figure 4.14   Top 15 stakeholders displayed in SWS

SIMS

The Stakeholder Information Management System (SIMS) is the database tool initially developed to support the *Stakeholder Circle* methodology. SIMS is a relational database that facilitates the recording, analysis and presentation of stakeholder information. Importantly, SIMS also allows the storage and comparison of stakeholder data through the life of an activity. The primary output of SIMS is the *Stakeholder Circle,* displayed in Figure 4.10. The application of *Stakeholder Circle* maps for sophisticated reviews and reporting has been described earlier.

Conclusion

The use of well-designed graphical representations is a valuable aid to understanding complex information. At the simplest level, analysing the data and then developing a diagram can aid the team in developing a deeper understanding of their stakeholder community. Preparation and presentation of stakeholder data through manual means, the SOAP template or the SWS worksheet achieves a similar outcome. The primary advantage of the SIMS database is its ability to automatically generate the **Stakeholder** *Circle* diagram and track changes over time. However, to achieve the maximum benefit for its use a level of organisational maturity is needed. Developing the skills and maturity needed by any organisation to optimise its stakeholder management is the subject for the third section of this book and Chapters 8 and 9.

This chapter provided guidelines on how to visualise and understand the information about the stakeholder community gathered from the first two steps of the **Stakeholder** *Circle* methodology. The final part of the process of building and maintaining robust relationships with the stakeholder community is the development and implementation of targeted communication strategies to facilitate successful engagement of these stakeholders for the benefit of the activity.

All relationships require constant work to maintain; this applies to family relationships, friendships, management of staff, and maintenance of professional networks. Relationships between an organisation and its stakeholders are no different. The team must understand the expectations of all stakeholders and how can they be managed through targeted communication. Chapter 5 will describe *step 4: engage,* and the process to develop targeted communication strategies and effective communication plans.

5

Measuring Stakeholder *Attitude*

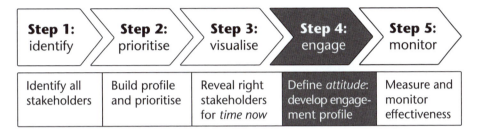

Figure 5.1   Chapter 5 focus

The final part of the process of building robust relationships with the stakeholder community is the development and implementation of targeted communication strategies. These strategies are essential for successful engagement of stakeholders to meet their expectations and for the benefit of the activity. Chapter 4 provided guidelines on how to present and understand the information about the stakeholder community gathered from the first two steps of the *Stakeholder Circle* methodology. This information can be used in many ways including:

- promoting the benefits derived from the activity's outcome;

- raising the profile of the activity or the profile of the organisation;

- gaining more attention for the execution or outcomes of the activity;

- announcing the membership of the stakeholder community to increase commitment of the community's members to the activity and its outcomes.

The information may also prove valuable in understanding the perceptions, fears and objections of stakeholders opposed to the activity to help mitigate or at least manage the opposition.

Any relationship requires constant work to maintain; this applies to family relationships, friendships, management of staff, and maintenance of professional networks. Relationships between an organisation and its stakeholders are no different. The team must understand the expectations of all of the important stakeholders and how they can be managed through targeted communication to maintain supportive relationships and to mitigate the consequences of unsupportive stakeholders for the benefit of the organisation and its activities. The structure of this chapter will be as follows: firstly a discussion of stakeholder engagement and a definition of *attitude*, and its component concepts of *support* and *receptiveness*; followed by the application of these concepts through *step 4: engage* of the **Stakeholder** *Circle* methodology leading to targeted communication strategies; and finally, some points about developing effective communication plans. Figure 5.1 shows the position of this *step* in the overall structure of the methodology.

Stakeholder Engagement

WHAT IS STAKEHOLDER ENGAGEMENT?

Definitions for *engagement* point to multiple approaches:[1]

- involvement or commitment to a cause or an idea, both:

  - emotional;

  - physical.

- participation in the actions of a group;

- intervention, intercession or conflict:

  - military battles;

  - fights.

- obligations or agreements, either social or financial:

  - mutual promise to marry;

---

1 http://www.visualthesaurus.com; http://dictionary1.classic.reference.com

- – contractual arrangements.

- employment, especially for a specified time.

The definition of stakeholder and the process of stakeholder identification from the multiple perspectives of *upwards, downwards, sidewards and outwards* within the **Stakeholder** *Circle* methodology supports this multi-dimensional view. Based on the diverse approaches to engagement listed above, *engagement can be defined as: practices, processes and actions that an organisation must perform to involve stakeholders in any organisational activity to secure their involvement and commitment, or reduce their indifference or hostility.*

The Institute of Social and Ethical Accountability (AccountAbility 2006: foreword), released a *Standard for Stakeholder Engagement* to 'promote… an innovative, multi-stakeholder governance model'. The Standard covers all areas of an organisation's affairs: external, internal and social. Examples are listed below:

- functional (external) engagements:

  - – customer care;

  - – public relations;

  - – supplier relations;

  - – regulatory and government relations.

- organisation-wide (internal) engagements:

  - – reporting and assurance;

  - – management accounting;

  - – HR management.

- issue-based engagement:

  - – human rights;

–   heritage and environmental moral rights;

–   philanthropic.

The Standard further proposes a three-part stakeholder engagement process:

- Learning the needs, expectations, perceptions of stakeholders and issues they may have, or may present, to the team responsible for the activity. These processes are equivalent to the *Stakeholder* Circle methodology's *step 1: identify* and *step 2: prioritise.*

- Innovating: incorporates the concept of 'drawing on stakeholder knowledge and insights to inform strategic direction and drive operational excellence' (AccountAbility 2006: 9). This is equivalent to the concept of *mutuality,* understanding a stakeholder's importance and stake in the outcomes of the activity. The stake can include *contribution* to the organisation or an activity through specialist or organisational knowledge, or financial or moral support, or feedback from external stakeholder groups on the impact or consequences of specific organisational actions.

- Performing: actually implementing the plans and strategies developed through stakeholder analysis and engagement activities; providing data to the activity for improvement but also providing data to stakeholders to enable them to assess the organisation's performance. This is equivalent to the *Stakeholder Circle* methodology's *step 4: engage* and *step 5: monitor.*

A DEFINITION OF *ATTITUDE*

Definitions for *attitude* are also multi-dimensional,[2] indicating that multi-dimensional approaches may be necessary when dealing with stakeholders and sustaining stakeholder relationships. The definitions can be categorised as follows:

- emotional:

---

2   http://www.thefreedictionary.com; http://www.visualthesaurus.com

- a state of mind or feeling;

- a negative approach to life;

- the result of perception, learning and experience.

- behavioural (either personal preferences or related to culture):

- tolerance;

- opinion;

- manner.

- receptiveness:

- willingness to engage;

- responsive to the needs of the activity;

- sympathetic and accessible;

- open to, and interested in, information about the activity, its progress, issues and outcomes.

APPLICATION OF *ATTITUDE* IN ORGANISATIONS TODAY

A stakeholder's *attitude* towards an organisation or any of its activities can be driven by many factors including:

- whether involvement is voluntary or involuntary;

- whether involvement is beneficial personally or organisationally;

- what the level of a stakeholder's investment is, either financial or emotional, in the activity.

If the individual or group's stake in the activity is perceived to be beneficial, or potentially beneficial to them, they are more likely to have a positive *attitude* to the activity and be prepared to contribute to the work to deliver it. If on the other hand, they see themselves as victims or losers, they will be more likely to hold a negative *attitude* to that activity. Part of the assessment of the stakeholder's *attitude* will be a review of the stake the stakeholder has, and his or her expectations and requirements for success or failure of the activity. The assessment will need to take into account the following elements that shape *attitude.*

ELEMENTS THAT SHAPE *ATTITUDE*

These can be categorised as follows:

- culture:

  - of the organisation doing the activity;

  - of a stakeholder organisation.

- identification with the activity and its outcomes:

  - personal values;

  - identification with the purpose or the activity.

- perceived importance of the activity and its outcomes;

- personal attributes:

  - personality;

  - position in the organisation.

This essential information can often be derived from the information gathered through the steps of the **Stakeholder** *Circle* methodology. However, further discussions may be necessary to complete the ratings for *step 4: engage.*

HOW TO GAUGE *ATTITUDE*

Step 4: engage is centred on identifying approaches based on stakeholder engagement profiles and tailored to the expectations and needs of stakeholders previously identified and categorised. Developing these engagement profiles constitutes the final step in the gathering of information about the stakeholder community necessary for effective communication. The engagement profiles are developed by:

- assessing the actual *attitude* of selected stakeholders;

- describing the optimal (or target) *attitude* of these stakeholders necessary for success of the activity.

The steps in this process are:

- Identify the current level of *support* of the stakeholder(s) at five levels: from *active support* (committed – rated as 5), through *neutral* (rated as 3), to *actively opposed* (antagonistic – rated as 1). Table 5.1 summarises these ratings.

- Analyse the current level of *receptiveness* of each stakeholder to messages about the activity: from *eager to receive information* (direct personal contacts encouraged – rated as 5), through *ambivalent* (rated as 3), to *completely uninterested* (rated as 1). Table 5.2 summarises these ratings.

Table 5.1   Ratings for *support*

Support	5. Active support: provides positive support and advocacy for the activity. 4. Passive support: supportive, but not actively supportive. 3. Neutral: is neither opposed nor supportive. 2. Passive opposition: will make negative statements about the activity, but not do anything to affect its success or failure. 1. Active opposition: is outspoken about opposition to the activity, and may even act to promote failure or affect success.

Table 5.2   Ratings for *receptiveness*

Receptiveness	5. High: eager to receive information. 4. Medium: will agree to receive information. 3. Ambivalent: may agree to receive information. 2. Not interested: not prepared to receive information. 1. Completely uninterested: emphatically refuses to receive information.

- Identify the optimal engagement position: the level of *support* and *receptiveness* that would best[3] meet the needs of both the activity and the stakeholder. If an important stakeholder is both actively opposed and will not receive messages about the activity, he or she will need to have a different engagement approach from stakeholder(s) who are highly supportive and encourage personal delivery of messages.

EXAMPLES OF ENGAGEMENT PROFILES

Figure 5.2 shows some examples of assessments of engagement profiles. Stakeholder 1 has been assessed as being *ambivalent* about the activity, neither supportive nor unsupportive (3), and *not really interested in receiving any information* about the activity (2). These results are shown by 'X' in the appropriate boxes in the matrix. However, the team has decided that the target *attitude* SHOULD BE *neutral* (3) and *ambivalent about information* (3); this is shown with a bold circle. In this assessment there is only a small gap between the stakeholder's current *attitude* and the *attitude* the team has agreed is essential for the success of the activity: the engagement profile is shown as being close to optimal.[4]

Stakeholder 2 has been assessed as *passive unsupportive* (2) and at a *medium level of interest* in receiving information about the activity (4). The engagement profile SHOULD BE *actively supportive* (5) and *eager to receive information at any time* (5). In this case, the gap between the current engagement profile and the optimal profile indicates that a high level of effort will be required to develop communication strategies for this stakeholder, to encourage their support and interest in information about the activity. Generally this level of support is only needed from key stakeholders such as the sponsor, steering committee, or a member of the steering committee.

Stakeholder 3 in Figure 5.2 has been assessed as being *neither supportive nor unsupportive* (3), but *eager to receive information any time* (5). The team has assessed that this stakeholder SHOULD BE at a level of *receptiveness* of

---

3   'Best' involves balancing what is realistically achievable against the importance of the stakeholder moderated by the amount of effort that team can allocate to the communication process.

4   It is not essential that all stakeholders have a high level of *support and receptiveness* toward the activity: part of the key decision the team has to make is whether the stakeholder in question is important enough to warrant any work necessary to achieve this high level of *support*. This information has been gathered through the analysis in *steps 1–3*.

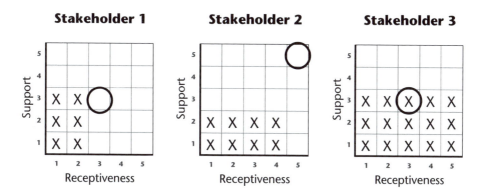

Figure 5.2   Engagement profile – stakeholders 1, 2 and 3

ambivalent: neither supportive nor non-supportive (3). This is a situation where the current profile is quite different from the optimal profile and will require careful handling from the team, to avoid alienating the stakeholder.

ANALYSIS OF STAKEHOLDER 3 EXAMPLE

Using the suggested guidance described later in this chapter, the options for closing the gaps for stakeholders 1 and 2 are not very complex. On the other hand there could be a number of paths to resolve the stakeholder 3 example:

- The stakeholder is a competitor, wanting to gather as much information about the activity as possible for the purpose of business intelligence. From the neutral level of support, this stakeholder is not dangerous to the success of this activity, but may be to other activities or to the organisation as a whole. If this is the case, whatever safeguards that can be put in place to reduce the amount of information available to the stakeholder should be done so immediately. It will be essential to repeat the assessment within a short framework to see if the tactics put in place have been successful.

- The stakeholder is a manager, not necessarily important to the success of the activity, but one who regularly requires lots of information. This may be from a power perspective – 'knowledge is power' – to raise his profile. It is essential to interview this stakeholder to offer him more targeted information, in recognition of his busy schedule. The offer should be in terms of quality of information rather than quantity, and perhaps the type of information his colleagues are receiving.

- He is unsure about the information he needs to know about the activity and so requires as much data as is available. The solution here is to meet with the stakeholder and re-affirm his stake in the activity and his expectations/requirements. Once again he may be searching for more specific details to try to extract information that he believes may be important.

In all cases, the team will want to reduce the amount of information being delivered to this stakeholder to reduce the workload of the team. However, it may be better to not change the amount of information if there is any suspicion that the stakeholder may be alienated by his perception of reduction in information, and therefore reduction in attention the team is paying. Alternatively the team may decide to reduce the information gradually, re-assessing *attitude* at more frequent intervals than normal.

WHEN CURRENT *ATTITUDE* IS EQUAL TO TARGET *ATTITUDE*

Figure 5.3 shows examples of stakeholders who have been assessed as having a correct engagement profile: the current *attitude* is *equal to* the target *attitude* necessary for success of the activity. These stakeholders have been assessed as exhibiting the appropriate level of *support and receptiveness* for success of the activity. It is important to note that the target *attitude* does not have to be at the level of stakeholder 5; for less important stakeholders a neutral profile, as shown for stakeholder 4 in Figure 5.3, will be a suitable target. Table 5.3 summarises the ratings for the stakeholder examples shown in Figure 5.2 and Figure 5.3.

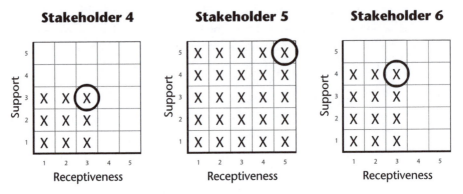

Figure 5.3   When current *attitude* is equal to target *attitude*

Table 5.3   **Analysis of stakeholder examples**

Stakeholder	Current support	Current receptiveness	Optimal support	Optimal receptiveness	Comments
1	3: neutral	2: not interested	3: neutral	3: ambivalent	Small gap between current and optimal, probably does not require action.
2	2: passive opposition	4: medium	5: active support	5: eager to receive information at any time	Large gap between current and target, will require additional communication effort to achieve desired *attitude*.
3	3: neutral	5: eager to receive information at any time	3: neutral	3: ambivalent	See section: Analysis of Stakeholder 3 Example.
4	3: neutral	3: ambivalent	3: neutral	3: ambivalent	This stakeholder is not assessed as being important for success, at this time in the activity.
5	5: active support	5: eager to receive information at any time	5: active support	5: eager to receive information at any time	This stakeholder is probably a senior manager assessed as being essential for success: maintain existing communication plan.
6	4: passive support	3: ambivalent	4: passive support	3: ambivalent	This stakeholder may naturally provide passive support for this and other activities for personal or management reasons without additional information.

Targeted Communication

Based on the overall level of engagement and the *mutuality* factors identified in *step 1*, a targeted communications plan can be developed focusing on:

- the key stakeholders;[5]

---

5   *Key stakeholders* are identified as having the power to damage the activity significantly, typically a power rating of 4. Key stakeholders are distinct from *important stakeholders* who have a

- other important stakeholders with a significant gap between their current *attitude* and the target *attitude*.

WHY TARGET COMMUNICATION?

In any activity the organisation decides to fund and support, the major constraints will be availability of resources, both human and financial. The timeframe for completion of the activity will usually provide an additional constraint. For these logistical reasons alone, the team will need to consider how best to manage its communication activities for maximum efficiency and effectiveness. However there are other more strategic reasons for a targeted approach to communication. Stakeholders who have been identified as essential to the success of the activity may be equally essential to other activities. Focused and relevant communication will have a better chance of a positive response than communication that is less focused and relevant. Analysis of who is important to the success of the activity will provide clear focus on the communication needs of these stakeholders. Finally, through a structured approach to understanding which stakeholders are most important, and what their expectations and *attitude* to the activity are, an understanding of potential conflicts between stakeholders' expectations of the activity can be exposed and addressed early.

COMMUNICATION PLANNING

The basis for an effective communication plan is to define for each stakeholder:

- the most appropriate information;

- the most effective message format; and

- the most efficient methods and frequency of transmission or delivery.

Figure 5.4 summarises the analysis of stakeholder communication strategic requirements. A stakeholder, once identified, is categorised into *directions of influence* to define the most appropriate format and content of the message; the central theme and intention of the message is influenced by *mutuality*, the

---

relatively high priority level; they are assessed as in the category of 'Top 5' or maybe 'Top 50', depending on the size of the overall stakeholder community.

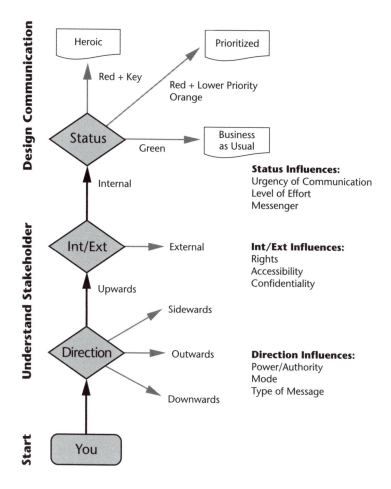

Figure 5.4   Stakeholder communication analysis: decomposition of *upwards*

two-way driver of successful relationships. Finally, the relative importance of each stakeholder (from *step 2: prioritise*) coupled with the engagement profiles (the matrix showing current *attitude* compared to target *attitude*) of these stakeholders will assist the team in establishing the most effective methods, and the quality, quantity and frequency of the messages.

THE MOST APPROPRIATE INFORMATION

Directions of influence (from *step 1: identify*) will help define the format and content of the message:

- *upwards;*

- *downwards;*

- *sidewards;*

- *outwards;*

- *internal* (to the organisation) or *external* (to the organisation).

THE MOST EFFECTIVE MESSAGE

Mutuality (from *step 1: identify*) will define the focus of the message, based on:

- why this individual or group has been selected as a stakeholder – why they are important to the success of the activity;

- what the stakeholder requires from success or failure of the activity – expectations or requirements.

If the message is crafted to give the stakeholder information that shows that his requirements are known and being considered, this will sustain a perception that the activity is well managed. The most appropriate messenger should be selected based on:

- who will be the most effective messenger – has the knowledge or experience;

- who is most likely to be listened to – is a peer of, or respected by the stakeholder;

- who can most effectively influence the attitude of the stakeholder?

THE MOST EFFICIENT METHODS

One of the most important aspects to consider is efficient delivery of the necessary information. The following guidelines provide the team with an understanding of where to focus their communication efforts. It is based on the analysis of engagement profiles described earlier in this chapter (*step 4: engage*), and by defining different levels of communication activities depending on whether the current engagement position:

- is *equal to* the optimal position (Figure 5.3);

- is *less than* the optimal position (see stakeholder 2 in Figure 5.2);

- is *greater than* the optimal position (see stakeholder 3 in Figure 5.2).

In the first instance where the current engagement position is *equal to* the optimal position, communication can be maintained at its current level: the defined level and frequency of regular reports, meetings, and presentations can be safely maintained. This might be flagged as 'green' in an organisation's reporting schema as needs are being met. For the situation where the current engagement position is *greater than* the optimal position, two possible approaches need to be considered, depending on the engagement profile. In Figure 5.2, stakeholder 3 is rated as being well above the level of *receptiveness* to messages necessary for success of the activity, but at the appropriate level of *support* of the activity to ensure success. The decision the team has to make regarding stakeholder 3 is whether to reduce the level of information flowing to this stakeholder (and risk a reduction in *support* from this stakeholder) or to maintain the current level of communication. The decision can only be made in the light of the knowledge the team has gained during the preceding steps of the stakeholder analysis.

For the third category where the current engagement profile is less than the target position and the stakeholder is relatively important, the team needs to focus their efforts on heroic communication: stakeholder 2 (Figure 5.2) is in this category. This type of communication is generally needed for only a small percentage of stakeholders, but any effort expended on increasing the levels of *support and receptiveness* to the optimal position will significantly benefit the activity. Generally in this case, a number of different communication approaches need to be used. These approaches could include regular reports and meetings, special presentations and possibly even using the influence of other important but supportive stakeholders to deliver essential information. Multiple complex communication activities must be coordinated by a relationship manager. This responsibility could be assigned to the manager of the activity, a functional manager or a supportive senior stakeholder. The different approaches just described are summarised in Table 5.4.

The Communication Plan

Based on each stakeholder's engagement strategy, a communication plan can be developed. The communication plan should contain:

Table 5.4   Targeted communication approaches

Engagement profile	Communication approach	Comments
Current *attitude* is equal to target attitude.	'business as usual': situation 'green'.	Existing communication package does not need to change.
Small gap between current *attitude* and target *attitude*.	'business as usual' +: situation 'amber'.	Existing communication package may require some small additional communication effort.
Current *attitude* is greater than target *attitude*.	See analysis on stakeholder 3.	Communication approaches need to be defined specifically for stakeholders in this group.
Current *attitude* is less than target *attitude*.	'heroic': situation 'red'.	Existing communication package may need to be significantly changed AND augmented by additional effort involving multiple approaches to ensuring more directed information about the activity is delivered to the stakeholder.

- stakeholder name and role;

- *mutuality*:

    - how the stakeholder is important to the activity;

    - the stakeholder's stake;

    - the stakeholder's expectations.

- categorisation of influence (*upwards, downwards, outwards, sidewards, internal* and *external*);

- engagement profile preferably in graphical form (see Figure 5.2):

    - level of *support* for the activity;

    - level of *receptiveness* to information about the activity;

    - target engagement: target levels of *support and receptiveness*.

- strategies for delivering the message:

    - *who* will deliver the message;

- *what* the message will be: regular activity reports or special messages;

- *how* it will be delivered: formal and/or informal, written and/or oral; technology of communication – emails, written memos, meetings;

- *when:* how frequently it will be delivered and over what timeframe (where applicable);

- *why:* the purpose for the communication: this is a function of mutuality – why the stakeholder is important for activity success, and what the stakeholder requires from the activity;

- *communication item:* the information that will be distributed that is, the content of the report or message.

EFFECTIVE COMMUNICATION

Communication is the primary tool for stakeholder engagement. The effectiveness of the communication is influenced by many factors including:

- the relationship between sender and receiver;

- other barriers to effective communication.

RELATIONSHIP BETWEEN SENDER AND RECEIVER

Irrespective of how well the communication strategy and plan are crafted, other factors must be considered:

- The different levels of power or influence between the team and the stakeholder: it may not be considered appropriate for an individual from the team to communicate with a stakeholder at a higher level in the organisation or the community outside the organisation:

    - ss a rule of thumb: the more powerful the stakeholder, the less detail and more focused the report or message should be.

    - know their preferences: does the powerful stakeholder prefer graphical representation, spreadsheets, or words?

- The role of the stakeholder:

  – sponsor or other political activity supporters may require exception reports, briefing data sufficient to be able to defend the activity; and *no surprises*;

  – middle managers who supply activity resources need timeframes, resource data and reports on adherence to resource plans and effectiveness of resources provided; more comprehensive information;

  – staff working on the activity and other activity team members need detailed but focused information that will enable them to perform their activity roles effectively;

  – other staff need updates on progress of activity, particularly information on how it will affect their own work roles;

  – external stakeholders will also require regular planned and managed updates on the activity, its deliverables, its impact, and its progress.

- Credibility of the messenger and the message: the more the team has worked to build trust and a perception of trustworthiness and competence the more readily a stakeholder will receive, and act on, information. Credibility of this nature takes time to develop and is often the result of previous positive experiences, a reputation for being trustworthy, or through being seen by stakeholders as delivering information in a proactive and timely manner, even if it is bad news.

- The relevance of the information to the recipient: the team must ensure that information is of interest to the stakeholder and delivered in a manner that is most easily read and absorbed.

- The format and content of the message: the most appropriate level of detail and presentation style will also assist in ensuring that information is received and responded to in the most suitable way.

OTHER BARRIERS

Some factors may act as barriers to effective communication: some of those listed below can be managed through accessing information already available through data collection within the *Stakeholder Circle* methodology itself. Other factors, such as environmental and personal distractions may be temporary. Awareness of these factors and their consequences may drive the timing and context of the communication activity.

- Personal reality: conscious and unconscious thought processes will influence how individuals receive and process any information they receive.

- Cultural differences: differences in communication requirements may be caused by cultural norms influencing the preferred style of presentation, content, delivery of information. These differences may be:

  - national;

  - generational;

  - professional;

  - organisational.

- Personal preferences: personality differences may also dictate the *how* and *what* of effective communication. A senior manager with limited available time and a preference for summary information will have no patience for information delivered as a story, whereas a team member or a stakeholder with a different personality style may find the delivery of facts not interesting enough.

- Environmental and personal distractions will include:

  - noise;

  - lack of interest;

  - fatigue;

> – emotions: if either the sender or the receiver is known to 'have a bad day', or is feeling unhappy, it is better to postpone any face-to-face communication until another occasion.

COMMUNICATING TO UNSUPPORTIVE STAKEHOLDERS

A stakeholder who has been identified as being supportive should not be ignored or taken for granted, but should be given the appropriate information in the manner that best suits that stakeholder's requirements. However, communication with stakeholders will require different techniques if they are:

- unsupportive and unreceptive (see stakeholder 7 in Figure 5.5);

- supportive but unreceptive (see stakeholder 8 in Figure 5.5);

- ambivalent and receptive (see stakeholder 9 in Figure 5.5);

- ambivalent and unreceptive (see stakeholder 1 in Figure 5.2).

A starting point should be:

- How supportive does this stakeholder need to be? Is it necessary that they are very supportive, or is it sufficient that they are just not unsupportive? A benchmark of optimal *support* needs to be defined for these stakeholders. It is not essential for all stakeholders to be very supportive; in some cases a neutral profile is sufficient.

- An analysis of the reason(s) for lack of *support* or *receptiveness*. This information should already have been documented in the stakeholder identification and prioritisation exercise(s):

    - If the stakeholder is unsupportive of this activity because he/she is supportive of another competing activity, negotiation needs to occur to resolve the competition. If the stakeholder will not negotiate, the activity managers should work together to resolve the issue.

    - If the stakeholder is too busy to receive information about the activity, and therefore will not read emails, or attend meetings, a number of options can be considered. Often busy managers

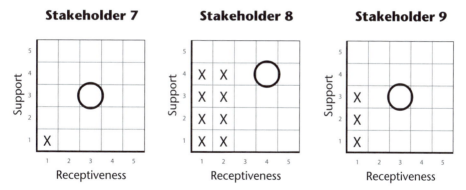

Figure 5.5 Engagement profile for stakeholders 7, 8 and 9

will take a break for an informal coffee meeting, if not with the manager then with someone else who can deliver information, or seek support on behalf of the activity. Another technique for delivering information to busy managers is to have it included into a management meeting that the stakeholder considers important enough to attend.

- A stakeholder, who is ambivalent but receptive to messages, may be prepared to act as a conduit to other stakeholders who are less receptive.

SPECIAL OR AD HOC REPORTS

Special or ad hoc reports are generally:

- a requested update on activity progress, because the activity is high profile, or is perceived to not be delivering according to plan;

- good news – activity delivered early, and/or within budget, a significant milestone has been achieved;

- bad news – the activity is slipping, costing too much, a known risk event has occurred but contingency plans were unsuccessful, an unknown risk has occurred.

The rules of content, format, messenger for regular reports will apply to these ad hoc reports.

SPECIAL GROUPS, BROADCAST OR GENERAL MESSAGES

In describing the actions necessary to develop a communication plan for appropriate communication to stakeholders, the focus has been on assuming that team members have access to their stakeholders. However, activities that an organisation initiates may impact large groups of stakeholders who are:

- globally dispersed;

- external organisations with contractual arrangements;

- potentially disadvantaged by the activity or its outcomes; or who

- require specialised information or specialised management.

In such cases, a corporate communications group must be briefed to prepare, manage and disseminate the messages on behalf of the team.

The discussions on preparation of messages to stakeholders has centred primarily on groups and individuals who have been prioritised as being relatively important to the success of the activity. It is essential to ensure that the stakeholders who are not considered as being in the relatively important category are not ignored. Such stakeholders will often merit broadcast or general messages. For example, a government body intending to resume land for public works or to renovate public buildings must ensure that notices of this intention are published in newspapers, to supplement other general messages.

IMPLEMENTING COMMUNICATION PLANS

The contents of the communication plan should be:

- available to all interested parties, especially activity stakeholders;

- able to be amended when activity conditions change;

- able to be monitored and measured.

The communication plan should state clearly *who* will deliver *what* message, *when* and under what circumstance to all identified stakeholders to the extent that the key communication points for each stakeholder and each messenger should be included in the activity schedule and reported against in activity team meetings.

CHANGES TO THE COMMUNICATION PLAN

When conditions change to the extent that the stakeholder community changes, it will be necessary to review and perhaps amend the communication plan to reflect any changes to the stakeholder community. The trigger points for making these changes will generally be:

- the activity moves from one phase to another;

- stakeholders change roles and no longer have an interest in or are no longer impacted by the outcomes of the activity;

- stakeholders leave the organisation.

There may be other triggers for change. These should be defined in the process documentation. Both the stakeholder management plan and the communication plan should be stored in a format that allows approved/agreed amendments to be easily recorded.

Conclusion

In this chapter, guidelines for building the communication plan have been developed using the information and the results of the team's analysis of their stakeholder community. The discussion of the diverse definitions of stakeholder engagement and *attitude* complemented other essential information such as importance, expectations and influence on the success of the activity gathered from the previous *steps* of the **Stakeholder** *Circle* methodology. From this, a targeted communication plan can be crafted for the most effective and efficient way to communicate, in order to build and maintain essential relationships. However, even though the plan is detailed and well supported from the information available about the stakeholder community, a plan that is not well implemented will not achieve the goals of engaging stakeholders for the benefit of the organisation and its activities. The next chapter will focus on monitoring and measuring the implementation and effectiveness of the team's communication efforts.

Monitoring the Engagement

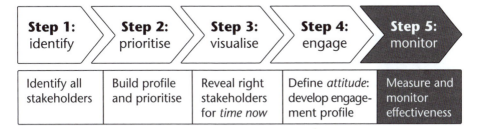

Step 1: identify	Step 2: prioritise	Step 3: visualise	Step 4: engage	Step 5: monitor
Identify all stakeholders	Build profile and prioritise	Reveal right stakeholders for *time now*	Define *attitude*: develop engage-ment profile	Measure and monitor effectiveness

Figure 6.1   Chapter 6 focus

The previous chapter described guidelines for building a communication plan based on the knowledge derived from the team's analysis of their stakeholder community. From these guidelines, a targeted communication plan can be crafted defining the most effective and efficient communication to build and maintain essential stakeholder relationships. However, this plan is only the starting point for engaging important stakeholders in the most appropriate way. To achieve an effective engagement of stakeholders for the benefit of the organisation, the plan must be implemented.

This chapter will focus on the actions necessary to ensure the communication plan has been executed: monitor the implementation, and measure the effectiveness, of the team's communication efforts. These activities are the essential parts of *step 5: monitor*, the final part of the *Stakeholder Circle* methodology. The structure of the chapter is as follows: discussions of the concept of the dynamic stakeholder community and requirements for maintaining a view of who are the right stakeholders at any time during the lifecycle of the activity. The second section describes key aspects of successful implementation of the communication plan and measuring its effectiveness. The final section discusses the importance of monitoring trends when measuring the effectiveness of the team's communication with its stakeholders. Figure 6.1 shows where this *step* fits into the **Stakeholder** *Circle* methodology.

Maintenance of the Stakeholder Community

The process of identifying, prioritising, and engaging stakeholders cannot be a once-only event. The work of managing relationships with stakeholders does not stop with planning. The nature and membership of the stakeholder community changes as stakeholders:

- are re-assigned;

- leave the organisation;

- assume different levels of relative importance to the activity;

- experience fluctuations in their power, interest or influence.

Also as the activity moves through its lifecycle or implementation stages, a stakeholder may have more or less impact on the activity. As a result, the process of re-assessing membership of the stakeholder community and the relationships within it may have to be repeated many times. An essential part of the monitoring process is the development of reviews and watching briefs to ensure that changes that affect the community and the relationships within it are detected and acted upon as soon as they occur or start to affect the success of the activity.

Monitoring the effectiveness of the communication plan

The process of monitoring the effectiveness of communication has three parts:

1. Ensuring that the communication plan is implemented;

2. Review of the stakeholder community to ensure that the membership is current – the right stakeholders for the current phase or time;

3. Review of the stakeholder engagement profile.

1. ENSURING THAT THE COMMUNICATION PLAN IS IMPLEMENTED

The strategy relating to the *who, what, when* and *how* of delivering the tailored messages defined for the important stakeholders must be converted into action.

Plans not implemented fail

Every methodology for managing projects and other organisational activities has a major focus on planning as an essential aspect of doing work. Planning describes the work, and incorporates research and decisions that the team must undertake in order to understand:

- what are the objectives of the work;

- what the team must do to achieve them;

- how they must do it;

- over what period of time it must be done;

- who should be involved;

- how its success will be measured and reported.

Without directions, instructions, milestones and reports, the team will waste time in fighting fires, in doing rework, and in last-minute negotiations to acquire suitable resources. This applies to communication plans as well as any other planning artefact the team develops.

The work of *step 5: monitor* includes implementing the planned communication action, and then monitoring and evaluating the results to understand the effects of the implementation and derive learnings. The communication plan is developed based on the information gathered through the four previous *steps* of the **Stakeholder** *Circle* methodology. *Step 5: monitor* is focused on processes to ensure the plan is implemented, the results of the communication activities are monitored and evaluated and the plan is revised where appropriate. This is the Deming cycle of *plan, do, check* and *act* (Tague 2004), the underlying basis of the doctrine of continuous improvement, a powerful concept that contributes to organisational learning and successful implementation of organisation activities.

Implementing communication plans for success

The communication plan should contain essential information to allow the team to use it to manage the *who, what, when* and *how* of communication with stakeholders. This information must be distributed to the team, to allow team members assigned with communication responsibilities to be clear on their assignment, but also to ensure that all members of the team are aware of these responsibilities. Once the communication plan has been developed and team communication responsibilities allocated, the principal communication points must be included in the schedule set up to manage the activity: a sample is shown in Figure 6.2 where delivery of regular reports such as the monthly report, the sponsor update and the cost report are recorded. Other events such as stakeholder reviews can also be included.

Including communication actions in the schedule will ensure a higher level of visibility of each team member's communication responsibilities and provide encouragement to those assigned to fulfil the responsibilities. Steps to achieving awareness are listed below:

- Document the plan.

- Allocate responsibility to those who are capable of doing the work. This means that members of the team will be given specific responsibilities for communication, not just the manager. However, the manager is responsible for coordinating and monitoring implementation of the communication plan.

- Ensure that all members of the team know their own and others' responsibilities.

- Include the communication plan in the schedule, a publicly available document.

- Monitor compliance regularly, ideally at a regular team progress meeting.

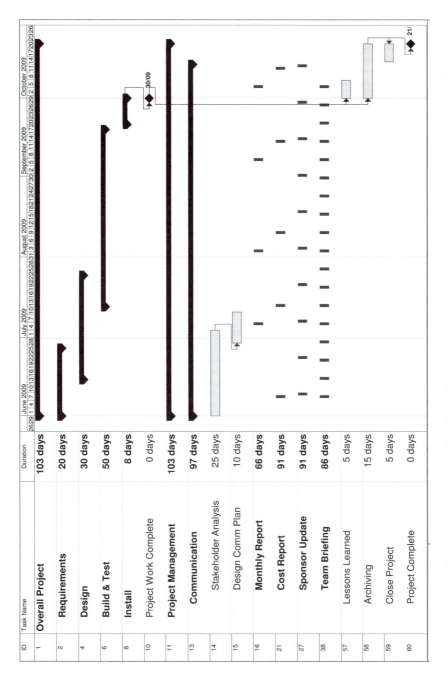

Figure 6.2   Example of communication sub-schedule

- Provide support and assistance to team members with communication responsibilities, particularly if they only have moderate experience in this area.

Monitoring this implementation

Including communication in the schedule means that team communication activities will be reported regularly at team meetings. This is the most regular and most effective form of monitoring, and ensures that team members will comply with their communication responsibilities through the application of peer pressure. From a positive perspective, reporting on communication effort on a regular basis has additional benefits:

- Other team members can learn from communication successes and failures.

- Information that may be collected through fulfilling communication responsibilities may be useful to the whole team. This statement applies whether it is just gossip about an impending change within the organisation, a change in personal circumstances of a particular stakeholder, or rumours of approval of new high-profile and therefore important rival activities. Even fragments of information may be parts of a jigsaw that other team members can contribute, to provide a more complete picture or be a trigger for further investigation, particularly if it means that progress or success of the activity is affected.

2. CONTINUOUS REVIEW OF THE STAKEHOLDER COMMUNITY

Part of the practice of continuous improvement and also the foundation of the *Stakeholder Circle* methodology is the understanding that successful implementation of an organisation's activities is through stakeholder relationship management. The key to managing these relationships is understanding that the stakeholder community is a network of people. It is not possible to develop relationships that will never change, just as it is not possible to make objective decisions about people. At best, a methodology should aim to reduce the subjectivity inherent in people making decisions about how to develop and maintain robust relationships with other people.

Because relationships are not fixed, it is necessary to review the membership of the stakeholder community regularly and continuously. This will ensure that, at all times throughout the implementation of any activity, the team has the most current information to manage the right stakeholders at that particular time. Regular reviews should be programmed:

- When the work of the activity moves from one stage of its implementation to the next: that is from planning to build, or build to implement.

- At regular intervals within a particular phase, if that phase is intended to go for a long time. A typical interval for this type of review would be three months.

The team also needs to continuously scan their stakeholder community for unplanned occurrences that may trigger a review when:

- The activity moves from one stage of its implementation to the next. For example: from planning the work to doing the work; or from doing the work to managing its implementation, to closing or completion.

- New personnel join the team.

Each time the dynamics of the stakeholder community change, membership of the community must be re-assessed.

3. REVIEW OF THE STAKEHOLDER ENGAGEMENT PROFILE

Each time the stakeholder community is re-assessed and the **Stakeholder** *Circle* updated, the corresponding engagement profile should also be reviewed and target *attitude* must be considered. This movement will provide an indicator of the effectiveness of the communication. Additional ad hoc reviews are triggered when the team observes an unexpected change in *attitude* in a key stakeholder.

Regular (planned) reviews

When the team meets for regular progress meetings, the communication schedule must be updated to reflect actual communication activity. The schedule should also include milestones to initiate a review of the engagement profiles of the key stakeholders. The process of review is a re-assessment of the ratings for *attitude*, consisting of assessing the current level of:

- *support;*

- *receptiveness.*

The current ratings are compared to the newly defined target *attitude* and any previous assessment, to measure any changes. It may also be necessary to re-evaluate these targets: if there has been a change in the importance of a stakeholder, the target *attitude* may need to be increased or decreased to reflect changes in that stakeholder's relative importance.

Some examples of results of reviews

Stakeholder 1 has been rated as the most important member of the community at this particular time. This stakeholder fits the profile of a government agency that is significant to the activity through its power to provide approvals. Like most government bodies it is neutral in *support* but requires more information (regular reports, other regulatory requirements). The first assessment of stakeholder 1 (see Figure 6.3) showed that there was not a large gap between the current attitude and the target *attitude.*[1] To maintain this relationship the team must provide any and all information necessary to meet the government's requirements, but also fulfil the team's need for the appropriate approvals. On the next scheduled review, the *attitude* of stakeholder 1 has reached the target. No new action will be necessary as a result of this review. A subsequent review, the third assessment, shows that the engagement profile is still at the optimal level, and this stakeholder is at the same level of importance – number 1: no additional communication effort is necessary under the current conditions.

Stakeholder 2 fits the profile of a senior manager in the organisation, perhaps the sponsor or a group such as the senior leadership team. It may also describe a stakeholder outside the organisation, such as a government minister, or a powerful lobby group. For stakeholder 2 (shown in Figure 6.4), the first assessment shows that *heroic*[2] communication efforts are required to

---

1   *Attitude* is the combination of ratings for *support* and *receptiveness*. The current *attitude* is shown by 'X' and the target *attitude* is shown with a bold circle. The engagement profile is the combination of current and target *attitudes* depicted in the 5 x 5 matrix.

2   *Heroic* communication has been described in the previous chapter as the highest level of communication activity required when there is a large gap between the current *attitude* and the target *attitude* of a key stakeholder.

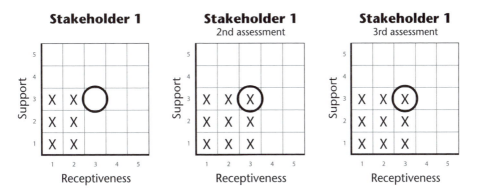

Figure 6.3   Results of review of attitude of stakeholder 1

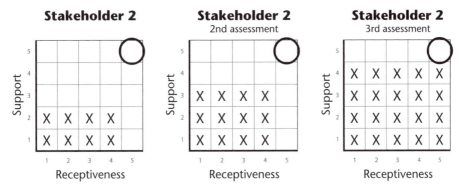

Figure 6.4   Results of review of attitude of stakeholder 2

close the gap between current and target *attitude*. In this case, the intention of any communication must be to increase the stakeholder's level of *support* and *receptiveness* to information about the activity, its progress and issues. The second assessment reveals that some progress had been made, but more work is necessary to achieve the desired level of engagement. The decision the team needs to make at this point is whether to continue at the same level of communication expecting a steady growth in this stakeholder's *attitude*, or to include additional techniques and messages to raise the levels of *support* and *receptiveness* to the desired level.

In the case of stakeholder 2, whatever the team decided to do, their efforts were moderately successful: the stakeholder was rated as *passively supportive*, where the target had been defined as *actively supportive*. The decision the team must make at this stage is whether to aim for the highest level of support, or be satisfied with the result achieved to date. This decision must be made in the context of the needs of the activity, the amount of available time and personnel that can be devoted to this task and whether the team can actually gain any more of the stakeholder's time and attention. The team may need to:

- Seek advice from other stakeholders with more knowledge and experience of the:

    - politics of the organisation; or

    - expectations of the stakeholder under consideration; or

- Draw on the combined knowledge and experience of its members to support decisions about whether to:

    - continue as planned; or

    - modify the communication plan or the target *attitude*.

Stakeholder 3 fits the profile of a functional or operational manager, requiring as much information as possible, because 'knowledge is power'. Stakeholder 3's engagement profile and possible solutions were discussed in the previous chapter. From data displayed in Figure 6.5, it appears likely that the team decided to consult with stakeholder 3 to offer more specific information to meet his/her management needs, thus possibly reducing the volume of information that had been previously required, and therefore reducing the workload of the team. The results of the second assessment indicate that the stakeholder was satisfied with the format, content and

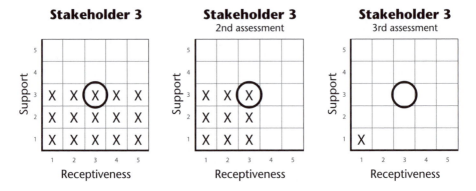

Figure 6.5   Results of review of attitude of stakeholder 3

volume of the communication provided. The team would probably have decided to continue this approach. The third assessment has shown that the stakeholder's *attitude* has regressed and he/she is no longer interested in the work of the activity. In fact, the stakeholder is actively opposed to the activity at this stage. There may be a number of reasons for this unexpected decline in *attitude* towards the activity. These reasons may not even be a reflection on the relationship between the team and the stakeholder. Other explanations for such a dramatic change could be:

- the stakeholder has been assigned to other work;

- the stakeholder has been demoted or otherwise lost power within the organisation;

- other activities have become more important;

- there may be personal issues preventing the stakeholder from being engaged with anything at work.

When changes to the stakeholder community occur

The situations described in the example of stakeholder 3 will often be outside the control of the team. They may be the result of:

- Organisational restructure where the organisation is reducing staff numbers, or reorganising to better meet the needs of the market.

- The stakeholder voluntarily decides to pursue opportunities outside the organisation.

- The changing nature of the market that the organisation operates in means that existing activities are frequently re-prioritised as other activities become more important and take precedence. This consequent re-prioritisation means that resources and funds may be reassigned to the new, more important activity. The result of the action may cause the attention of stakeholders will be re-focused onto this new activity.

- Organisational life and its activities do not operate in a vacuum. Individuals within the organisation will be affected by situations and conditions outside the organisation, tragic or joyful. These situations may cause the stakeholder to be less interested in any organisational issues, let alone issues that affect the activity's successful continuance.

The results of the third assessment for stakeholder 3 in Figure 6.5 shows a possible situation that could fit into any of the categories just described. The team should try to define the cause of the change and then plan an appropriate response based on their knowledge of the actual people and circumstances.

When relative importance is reduced

Figure 6.6 is an example of a situation where stakeholder 5, the fifth most important stakeholder at the first assessment, has been re-prioritised to 21 in the rankings as a result of a review of the membership of the stakeholder community. One explanation of this re-prioritisation could be that stakeholder 5 is a government minister whose portfolio covered the work of the activity at the first assessment, but has moved to another portfolio by the time of the second assessment. The first assessment shows that stakeholder 5 had been assessed as being actively supporting, and very receptive to information about the activity. The team had also assessed that this was the *attitude* necessary for success of the activity, and agreed that the current communication strategy for this stakeholder was sufficient. By the second assessment the stakeholder's *attitude* towards the activity had sunk to passively antagonistic (had no interest) for *support,* and not at all interested for *receptiveness.* If team members were previously aware of the

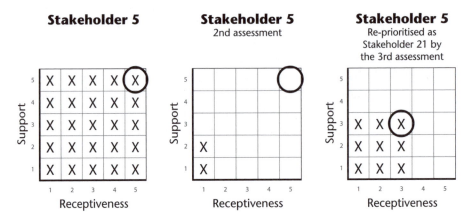

Figure 6.6   When a stakeholder is re-prioritised

changing situation, this result confirms what they had learned through other means. With this confirmation, the team has enough data to act. The action should begin with the re-prioritisation of the stakeholder community and the review of engagement profiles for stakeholders who have been affected by this situation. In this case, the team has reduced the targeted attitude to reflect the change of the stakeholder's situation and the nature of the relationship with the activity and the team. In addition, the team will modify its communication approach to meet the stakeholder's changed potential for impacting the success of the activity.

However, the team may not be aware of the change to the stakeholder's situation. This may have occurred because this stakeholder, while very important to the success of the activity, was not part of the organisation. The changes to the stakeholder's situation have occurred outside the organisation and will only become apparent during a review. In this case the result of the second assessment has acted as a trigger for the team to gather more data. With the resulting information and the confirmation of these results, the team can decide on the appropriate actions.

Once the stakeholder's ranking in the stakeholder community has changed, the target *attitude* been revised, and consequent changes made to the communication strategy, a further assessment must be done. The third assessment for this stakeholder shows that the relationship with this stakeholder, once modified to meet the changing circumstances, is as successful within its modified parameters as was recorded in the first assessment.

Figure 6.6 shows how a permanent change to a stakeholder's circumstances may be managed. Temporary, but not necessarily trivial, changes such as changes to a stakeholder's life outside the organisation may be reflected in the changes to a stakeholder's engagement profile. Figure 6.7 shows what might happen to a stakeholder's *attitude* through personal issues such as marriage, divorce, birth of a child or death of a close family member.

The profile shown in Figure 6.7 indicates that stakeholder 10 could be a key user involved in implementation at a later stage of the activity, either internal or external to the organisation. The team needs this moderate level of *support* for the activity at this (early) stage, but is motivated to provide the stakeholder with information in preparation for his or her involvement later. As the work moves closer to the relevant stage of implementation and

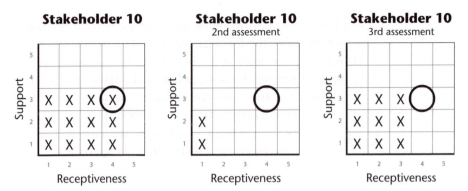

Figure 6.7   When personal circumstances affect a stakeholder's attitude

completion, higher levels of *support* and *receptiveness* will be necessary. The first assessment shows that stakeholder 10 has the target *attitude* necessary for the right relationship between the stakeholder and the activity at this stage of the activity. On the second assessment, without any warning, the stakeholder's *attitude* has become one of not caring at all about the activity. *This result will trigger an investigation.* In this example further investigation has disclosed that the stakeholder is dealing with a personal situation. The team must manage this challenging situation as sensitively and patiently as possible. There will be no need to change the target; the situation is most likely of a temporary nature. The team's expectation is that the stakeholder will resume duties once the personal situation has been resolved. The third assessment shows that the stakeholder is back at work and again part of the stakeholder community, and while *attitude* is not yet at the same level as it was in the first assessment, the trends indicate that by the next assessment the relationship will be at the appropriate level defined for success of the activity.

Ad hoc reviews

Ad hoc reviews will occur outside the regular review schedule. They will often be the result of information gathered by the team about the circumstances of a member of the stakeholder community. A review may be triggered by:

- information such as that described in Figures 6.6 or 6.7;

- a requirement for a health check on the progress of this activity or a programme that this activity contributes to;

- an enquiry based on specific stakeholders and their relationships with all activities being conducted in the organisation.

Whatever the reason for the review, the process will be similar: the ad hoc assessment is compared to the previous assessment, the data is reviewed and actions will be defined depending on the purpose of the review itself. A follow-up review must also be scheduled to ensure that the actions have delivered their intended outcome.

The examples shown in Figures 6.3 to 6.7 indicate multiple variations of responses that the team will need to consider and implement to maintain the necessary relationships. In any relationship, effort is required to build and maintain a relationship that matters, whether family, friends, colleagues or stakeholders. Complex responses to situations are often required. Guiding the team in making decisions on how to respond, and the act of responding itself requires leadership.

Leadership

An effective leadership style depends on a follower's ability (and willingness) to follow a leader; and depends on the power relationships between leader and those led. In the context of leadership in stakeholder practices within an organisation the following points are important to note:[3]

- Success of the activity is defined by its stakeholders.

- Effective communication is the only way to manage stakeholder expectations – unrealistic expectations are unlikely to be realised.

- The overall process is focused on win–win: an activity cannot be successful if any important stakeholders believe they have lost power or any other type of advantage because of the activity.

- Stakeholder management and risk management are closely aligned processes.[4]

---

3 See Chapter 1 for discussion of the importance of people to success and perceptions of success.
4 Please refer to the discussion in Chapter 1.

SKILLS AND KNOWLEDGE TO MANAGE RELATIONSHIPS

Successfully managing relationships in an organisation is a mixture of the *art* of leadership and the *craft* of management, requiring a balance of *management* and *leadership* within the environment of the stakeholder community.

Figure 6.8 shows how essential skills work together. Successful completion of an activity's deliverables depends on management of both *hard* skills – the control of time, cost and scope – and *soft* skills relating to leadership and relationship management. Hard skills are part of the *craft* of management and are the first dimension. The second set of skills is described as the *art* of leadership (see Figure 6.8). Soft skills are required to facilitate the application of hard skills because it is people who realise activities and not techniques or hardware. There is a third set of skills essential for successful delivery of activities; this is *flow*, requiring competencies beyond managing and leading.

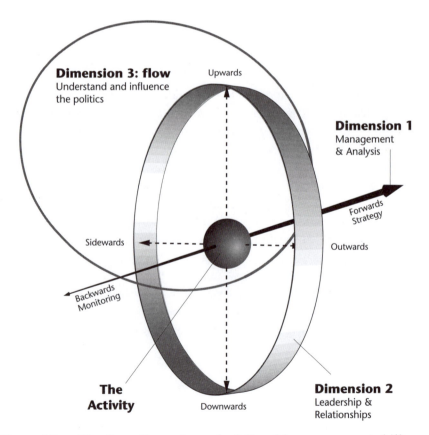

Figure 6.8   The three dimensions of relationship management skills

The key to *flow* is the ability to read the power structures of the organisation and its surroundings, and the willingness to operate in this environment. Based on the concepts developed by Csikzentmihalyi (1991), *flow* describes the conditions necessary for producing the perfect swing (golf) or the perfect note (music). This 'perfection' is the result of the confluence of natural talent and experience (or years of practice). *Flow* is not consistent or predictable: but a golfer or a singer 'knows' when he or she has 'hit the sweet spot'. Applied to management it is a skill/intuition that experienced and knowledgeable managers will bring to operating in the political environment of an organisation. Managers may develop these skills and acquire the appropriate experience and *wisdom* to manage within the organisation's political environments. Part of this skill-set is the ability to understand:

- the organisation's culture;

- the power bases operating within them;

- the expectations and perceptions of important stakeholders; and

- the development of strategies to ensure their support.

These concepts are defined in more detail in Bourne and Walker (2003).

Managing relationships that do not fall neatly into methodologies of management are the *flow* skills. In organisations this is understood as *politics*. It is dangerous to ignore the effect of politics on the outcomes of an activity, and important to understand how the patterns of political activity operate in and around any particular organisation. Understanding the power environment within the organisation and the position of those within it for particular issues is critical. It requires knowledge of the environment and all the stakeholders in this process and what their needs and wants are. Without formal power, the manager must to be able to influence people and outcomes.

The political tools that a manager should be capable and willing to use to ensure success include:

- gaining and maintaining support such as the sponsorship of a powerful champion;

- building alliances;

- controlling a critical resource, or the decision process, or the committee process through the agenda, membership and minutes;

- use of positional authority such as rewards or coercion; training, information or favours.

These tools are essential components for success. The theme of stakeholder relationship management is that communication is the key to successful distribution of information and wielding of influence.

Monitoring Trends

As noted earlier in this chapter, it is not possible to develop a methodology that is able to objectively measure the relationships between an activity and its stakeholders. The process of this methodology and every other methodology that attempts to define relationships depends on one group of people making decisions about the needs, requirements and attitudes of other people. There are two issues:

1.   Peoples' needs, requirements and attitudes do not remain fixed.

2.   We cannot read the hearts and minds of others no matter how empathetic we believe we are, or how close our relationship is with them.

Rather than attempt to measure absolutes, trend reporting is commonly used for measuring intangible or unmeasurable data, through measuring progress, such as actual against planned or other changes usually assessed against the first record – the baseline. Through a comparison of each new set of data against the baseline, or previous sets of data, the changes or differences will provide an indication of the success or otherwise of what is being measured.

The data collected through *step 5: monitor* provides the way to measure changes over time against a baseline. In the examples shown in this chapter the baseline is the first engagement profile. A second, and any subsequent measure of the engagement profile, always rated from the same set of statements, can be compared to the baseline. Progress or lack of progress, in building that relationship can be understood through the changes from the baseline data. This can be seen at the individual level using the engagement profile matrix used in Figures 6.3 to 6.7. The **Stakeholder** *Circle* database provides an aggregate report for the activity, showing the changes of each stakeholder but within the total environment of the activity – see Chapter 9 and Figure 9.3.

Conclusion

This chapter looked at the essential aspect of monitoring the communication plan developed for the current stakeholder community. The data used to build this plan was based on information gathered on members of that community through the first four *steps* of the **Stakeholder** *Circle* methodology. The team analysed this information and developed a targeted communication plan. Monitoring the efforts of building and maintaining stakeholder relationships requires constant scrutiny as the plan is implemented.

Communication is itself a human endeavour, and the complex communication that may be necessary for managing stakeholder relationships within an organisation or around its activities requires planning, monitoring and also leadership. The team must apply analysis, skills and experience to succeed in its complex communication efforts, and must exhibit leadership through proactive communication approaches and willingness to operate in the power structures of the organisation and its surroundings.

Finally trend reporting is described as being useful to understand the effectiveness of the communication strategies and to provide foundation data to enable the team to continue to manage fluctuating relationships and its dynamic community successfully.

Just as communication plans must be implemented in a planned and measured way, it is also essential to discuss ways to implement stakeholder relationship management and the **Stakeholder** *Circle* methodology in a sensitive and sustainable way. The Stakeholder Relationship Management Maturity (SRMM) model will be introduced in the next section of this book as a means to achieve sustainable and appropriate implementation of a methodology that matches the current level of level of readiness of any organisation to implement stakeholder relationship management processes and practices. This is achieved by understanding the level of readiness of an organisation, applying appropriate levels of implementation of stakeholder relationship management, and measuring success of that implementation.

SECTION III

Implementation

Section III provides guidelines to assist an organisation in the effective implementation of stakeholder relationship management processes and practices. The guidelines are in the form of Stakeholder Relationship Management Maturity (SRMM), a maturity model that helps an organisation identify its current level of readiness to implement a stakeholder relationship management methodology. When an organisation understands its own level of readiness, it can increase the chances of a successful implementation of stakeholder relationship management methodology by selecting appropriate aspects of the methodology to implement next. Too much change, and the change effort is wasted; too little and the change is ignored: 'we are already doing this!'

There are three chapters in this section:

- Chapter 7: Effective Implementation – describes conditions necessary for:

    - use of the *Stakeholder* Circle methodology to build and maintain relationships with stakeholders;

    - information that can be used to develop a business case for implementation of stakeholder relationship management in an organisation;

    - effective implementation of the methodology in an organisation;

    - a transition from using the *Stakeholder* Circle methodology for the success of an individual activity to organisation-wide implementation of the methodology.

- Chapter 8: Defining Organisational Readiness

  – defines the theoretical foundation of SRMM;

  – describes SRMM levels;

  – describes the types of organisation that would fit these levels.

- Chapter 9: Implementation Guidelines – implementing stakeholder relationship management processes and practices:

  – describes practical guidelines for moving from one level to another;

  – describes a process for supporting the accompanying change management activities with stakeholders impacted by the implementation of the new stakeholder relationship management processes and practices.

7

Effective Implementation

This chapter describes elements necessary for the successful implementation of the *Stakeholder* Circle in an organisation. Many of the ideas and discussions included in this chapter have already been described earlier in this book. For maximum usefulness to an organisation attempting to implement this methodology, they are summarised here. The chapter is organised as follows: first a summary of the value of the *Stakeholder* Circle methodology to an organisation. This is followed by a discussion of factors for successful use of the methodology at the activity level. Finally, factors for successful implementation at an organisational level are discussed as a transition to Chapter 8's discussion of maturity models, and their application in stakeholder relationship management.

Value of Stakeholder Engagement Methodology

The value of using a structured stakeholder management methodology, and in particular the *Stakeholder* Circle, can be considered from a number of different perspectives:

- the organisation;

- the stakeholders;

- the activity itself;

- the activity's manager and team.

Each of these perspectives is described in more detail.

VALUE TO THE ORGANISATION

Chapter 1 discussed how people (stakeholders) are crucial to the successful delivery of any organisational activity. Successful activities are those whose important stakeholders perceive them to be successful. The identification of the right stakeholders and the development of targeted communication to meet the needs of the activity and the expectations of stakeholders, will lead to a higher level of commitment and support from these stakeholders.

Stakeholders are more likely to support activities that they think will succeed; and are more likely to withdraw support from activities that they perceive are not succeeding. Therefore, it is essential to communicate relevant information to important stakeholders to provide them with the perception the activity is being well managed. This can be achieved through targeted communication that is aligned with their expectations and their information requirements.

If key stakeholders are committed to the success of the activity and fulfil their responsibilities to contribute to its success, the organisation will achieve additional value through:

- higher chance of *on time/on budget* delivery;

- ability to achieve business strategies more effectively.

ON TIME/ON BUDGET DELIVERY

Delays to implementation of activities usually occur through:

- essential senior management approvals being delayed;

- sponsor advocacy not provided when it is needed;

- promised resources not supplied when needed;

- supplier delivery promises not met;

- other people-related issues.

The result will often be that the activity's progress is delayed though hidden agendas within the organisation. If stakeholders are more engaged, and committed to a particular activity, and their communication needs are being met there is less chance that these issues will negatively impact progress of the activity. Delays to the work will incur additional expenditure, and impact the budget.

ACHIEVING BUSINESS STRATEGIES

Research has shown that organisations that have aligned their projects and other activities to their business strategies tend to be more successful financially (KPMG 2005). This means that decisions about:

- what activities should be given approval to proceed;

- how resources (funds and people) are allocated;

- how frequently the work of the activity is reviewed;

are made within the leadership team and are based on alignment to the organisation's current business strategies. Engagement of these decision-makers will be enhanced through provision of the information they need for assurance that the outcomes of the activity will continue to contribute to the organisation's business strategies.

VALUE TO THE STAKEHOLDERS

People (stakeholders) are essential to the successful delivery of the activity and its outcomes.[1] Building and maintaining robust relationships and maintaining an appropriate level of communication to stakeholders will ensure that:

- they receive information they require;

- they are consulted;

- their needs and requirements are 'heard', and where possible, actioned.

---

1   Chapter 1 – see discussion of Heathrow Terminal 5.

VALUE TO THE ACTIVITY

Alignment of risk management practices and stakeholder relationship management practices highlight the significance of managing relationships for success.[2] Engagement can be achieved through:

- understanding:

    - who is key and who is important in a dynamic environment;

    - how best to deliver essential information to engage the stakeholders.

- feedback on work that is being done or should be done to successfully deliver the activity – communication *from* the stakeholder;

- early warning about impending events or decisions that may affect the success of the activity – also communication *from* stakeholders;

- effective handling of (people) risk through targeted communication.

VALUE TO THE TEAM

Both the team and the team's manager will benefit from the application of stakeholder relationship management processes and practices in the following ways:

- they learn about operating more effectively as a team;

- they gain a sense of achievement through more successful communication and stakeholder engagement;

- they learn more:

    - from each other through discussion and consultation;

    - through working with stakeholders who know more about the subject, the politics, and the environment.

---

2   Chapter 1 – people and their actions are the main source of risk for any activity.

How Stakeholder Engagement Methodologies Contribute

Methodologies can contribute to success and therefore add value in the ways just discussed through:

- structure;

- support for decision-making;

- performance reporting;

- issue management.

STRUCTURE

A structured approach such as the 5 *steps* of the **Stakeholder** *Circle* methodology provides the team with assistance in stakeholder relationship management through:

- Providing a structure to enable the team to gather information about the relationship as the activity moves through its planning and subsequent phases.

- Easy progression from *step 1: identify* to *step 5: monitor*. While there are guidelines about information collection that best suit the specific steps of the methodology, progression to the next *step* is not dependent on gathering all the information defined on the previous *step*. It is essential however, to have gathered all the necessary information *before* developing and implementing the communication plans;

- Applicability to all types of organisational activities. Any activity that involves people and groups of people within and outside the organisation benefits from the application of a stakeholder relationship management methodology. The structure enables the team to develop a consistent means to communicate effectively with important stakeholders.

- The process of data collection and analysis is incremental, meaning that each set of information has a better chance of being valid. This approach is in contrast to stakeholder relationship management process and practices that require large leaps of judgement about stakeholders without a structured foundation to assist them.

- Managing stakeholder relationships and gathering essential data for communication can also be successfully developed as an incremental process when an organisation or team uses a selection of the *steps* in the early stages of its use within an organisation. From a pragmatic perspective, it is better for the team to focus on a few aspects of stakeholder relationship management, be successful with that selection of processes, and then retrofit other *steps* when the team is ready to do so. This pragmatic approach is the basis for SRMM which will be described in detail in Chapter 8.

SUPPORT FOR TEAM DECISION-MAKING

The application of any methodology in a consistent manner provides a more effective means for successfully implementing work in an organisation. This is particularly so with stakeholder relationship management. As has been stated earlier, making decisions about other people is difficult and in a business situation, no one person can know enough about another to guarantee effective communication and relationship management. The *Stakeholder* Circle methodology, with its emphasis on team decision-making and team allocation of communication responsibilities, attempts to minimise subjectivity through insistence on team reviews and also through emphasis on the consistent set of ratings for different attributes of each stakeholder. The methodology encourages a team focus (not the individual heroic approach) through the following:

- the team contributes to the analysis (*identify, prioritise, engage*);

- members of the team will be assigned communication tasks;

- members of the team are encouraged to participate in analysis and decisions about managing stakeholder relationships.

This consistent foundation for decision-making also assists the team through an emphasis on regular reviews and documentation of decisions about managing stakeholder relationship. Chapter 4 described the tools available:

- paper-based or MS Word templates to gather historical information about each stakeholder, whether individual or groups;

- a worksheet or database that can assist with providing:

  - guidance on information to be gathered at each *step*;

  - assistance in calculations;

  - storing data on each review to support trend analysis and other reporting;

  - more effective and time-efficient means to make changes to the stakeholder community when necessary.

PERFORMANCE REPORTING

Performance reporting in stakeholder relationship management has two main streams:

- trend analysis;

- documentation and audit trails.

Trend analysis has already been discussed.[3] The previous discussions can be summarised:

- It is not easy to gather data about people (stakeholders).

- It is not possible to make objective statements about people (stakeholders).

- In the **Stakeholder** *Circle* methodology the baseline will be the first engagement profile developed in *step 4: engage,* or the

---

3   Chapter 6 – trend analysis is useful when measuring intangibles.

first engagement profile developed after a major change in the importance of a stakeholder (see Figure 6.6 in Chapter 6).

- Subsequent assessments can show effects of team effort over a measured period of time through changes in the gap between current *attitude* and target *attitude*, in the engagement profile of a stakeholder.

Documentation storage and audit trails are essential for effective management of any activity. Documentation also serves as history for new team members to learn about the activity and its stakeholders. Audit trails are essential for 'health checks' and other evidence of efficient management of the activity and its stakeholders. The essential elements of documentation and its benefits are summarised as follows:

- The **Stakeholder** *Circle* methodology produces records of information gathered about stakeholders for the entire time the activity is being worked on.

- Graphics produced from *step 3: visualise* and *step 4: engage* provide records that are easy to create and interpret.

- Comments can be included in stakeholder data.[4]

ISSUE MANAGEMENT

Issues that will affect the successful delivery of the activity will fall into the following categories:

- Changes to the organisation, or the environment outside the organisation that will affect the activity, the team and its stakeholders. These should have been considered through risk management and if they occur the appropriate risk management strategy should be invoked:

  - changes to structure or leadership;

---

4   It is important that the team is aware of the need to ensure that all records maintained about stakeholders are always expressed in business language. No personal remarks should ever be recorded. It is also important to consider privacy and confidentiality issues when discussing circumstances of stakeholders and recording information about them. The ratings that have been allocated will usually provide sufficient detail for audit trails of decisions made and communication implemented for stakeholders.

- changes of government;

- re-adjustment of organisation budgets that will affect the activity's budget.

- Conflict:

    - within the team;

    - between the team and its stakeholders;

    - between key stakeholders.

- Misunderstandings or miscommunications, leading to the need to resolve the ensuing conflict through negotiation or conflict resolution.

The first category may be able to be managed through risk management strategies, or intensive communication campaigns to try to restore equilibrium for the activity. The other two categories require negotiation, conflict resolution or other types of specialised communication to resolve. Information collected about stakeholders and the environment of the activity can be very useful in preparing for these specialised communications. The following structure is also useful as a basis for resolving conflict, raising issues to senior management for their consideration and resolution or negotiation.

AN APPROACH FOR ISSUE RESOLUTION

- Know what the issue (really) is. The team should be able to describe it in one short sentence.

- Know what an acceptable resolution is – also described in a short sentence.

- Define (multiple) steps to achieve this acceptable resolution.

- Use the data collected about the stakeholders and the environment.[5]

---

5   This approach is also useful for briefing senior management about issues that concern them and particularly when action is needed from senior management for the resolution of the issue.

The following section will focus on the factors necessary for successful use of stakeholder relationship management to ensure successful implementation of the activity.

Successful Use of the Methodology for an Activity

The factors essential for successful application of the *Stakeholder* *Circle* methodology for an activity's stakeholder relationship management are:

- committed team;

- committed senior management;

- careful selection of projects or other activities for its initial introduction;

- long-term strategic use;

- central support, such as a Programme (or project) Management Office (PMO);

- universal application;

- consistent use across the organisation;

- outputs considered as guidelines for decisions.

COMMITTED TEAM

The commitment and loyalty of individual members of the team are enhanced through inclusion of the team in:

- decision-making;

- work to engage stakeholders;

- knowledge-sharing about stakeholders and the political environment.

COMMITTED SENIOR MANAGEMENT

Research shows that projects (or other organisational activities) can only succeed with the overt, sustained support from senior management.[6] Support can take the form of:

- advocacy with peers in the organisational hierarchy for survival of the activity in the political environment;

- involvement through high levels of *support* and *receptiveness*;

- consistent funding;

- consistent supply of appropriate resources (people and other) to the work of the activity.

CAREFUL SELECTION OF ACTIVITIES

It is important to carefully select activities in the early stages of implementation of the *Stakeholder* Circle. Generally, high-profile projects, programmes that are universally recognised as connected to delivering business strategy, marketing or change programmes are ideal candidates for early adoption. Single implementation of structured stakeholder management methodology such as *Stakeholder* Circle methodology requires:

- strategic (not tactical) focus;

- the team's acceptance of the need to regularly review the membership of the stakeholder community;

- sufficient personnel to manage planning, implementation and reporting on stakeholder engagement activities;

- ancillary support, such as project administration staff to take some of the administration load off the team;

- budget sufficient to incorporate these additional personnel and responsibilities.

---

6   Chapter 1 – factors for successful change in an organisation.

Long-term strategic activities are preferred because early focus of a consistent process for stakeholder relationship management should be strategic for the following reasons:

- Projects (particularly small projects) are essentially *tactical* and often do not have sufficient capacity to continue reviews of stakeholder community:

  - Team members tend to get caught up in the tactical issues and conflicts, and may neglect or postpone the essentially strategic reviews of the stakeholder community.

  - Generally project managers of these small projects do not have the experience and knowledge to understand the need to maintain relationships.

- Long timelines allow team members to incorporate culture of stakeholder relationships into team practices:

  - through the experience of what happens when stakeholders are engaged and/or neglected;

  - through observing the actions of more experienced team members or peers.

CENTRAL SUPPORT (PMO)

A central support unit such as a PMO is essential for the support of an implementation of processes and practices. PMOs can assist with facilitation of team decision-making in areas such as:

- initial identification and analysis of stakeholders;

- decision-making on resolution processes for issues that may occur;

- providing training;

- centralised expertise;

- support for the tools in use;

- documentation development, storage and retrieval.

UNIVERSAL APPLICATION

Stakeholder relationship management is an appropriate discipline to support many organisational activities, whether corporate social responsibility (CSR) activities, marketing or change management or projects to deliver business strategy. Such diverse use is beneficial to an organisation because:

- Project management disciplines are now the accepted way for organisations to deliver projects, programmes and other activities to achieve business strategy.

- Project managers and project teams may not necessarily have knowledge, experience or resource capacity for managing stakeholder engagement.

- Other organisation activities often are directed or managed by more senior and experienced people who understand the importance of relationship maintenance in the following activities:

  - marketing;

  - sales;

  - competitor analysis;

  - mergers and acquisitions;

  - account management (organisational relationship management);

  - change management;

  - supply chain managers;

  - strategic planners.

CONSISTENCY OF APPLICATION OF PROCESSES AND PRACTICES

The more consistent practices and processes, the more efficient the organisation through:

- a single set of training;

- a central pool of experts;

- effective transfer of personnel from one activity to another;

- application of *lessons learned* to the whole of an organisation's endeavour (if shared).

Factors for Successful Implementation at an Organisational Level

Successful implementation of change programmes involving new processes and practices such as implementation of stakeholder relationship management within an organisation require consideration and application of the following factors:

- The effort of implementation should be aligned with the ability and capacity of the organisation to absorb the change.

- Its introduction should be treated as a change programme, and managed with project disciplines.

- A business case defining the benefits to be achieved must be developed, approved and sponsored by a senior champion.

IMPLEMENTATION ALIGNED WITH READINESS

The introduction of new processes and practices needs to be aligned with the capacity and capability of an organisation, and its personnel, to accept any impacts of this change. This is the readiness of the organisation, and will vary with each organisation. Therefore for the successful implementation of the new processes and practices contained within the **Stakeholder** *Circle* methodology, it is essential to match the implementation programme with the organisation's ability to absorb the new processes and practices:

- If the processes and practices to be introduced are too advanced or too complex, it is likely to generate a high level of resistance resulting in a reduced chance of successful implementation of the change.

- If the processes and practices to be introduced are perceived to be similar to existing processes and practices, resistance may take the form of 'We are already doing this, why would we change?'

It is also essential to be able to measure benefits of improvements initiated through implementation. The following is a suggestion on the process to accomplish measurement of the implementation effort:

- Establish a baseline (define a start date of the improvement programme).

- Measure progress through stages of improvement (achievement of agreed milestones against the plan developed for the improvement).

- Track effort to provide the basis for subsequent business cases for further extension or more, deeper implementation (measure effort and resources for this task as a specific project or activity within a project).

- Track expenditure and effort expended to do so (measure of cost of the effort).

The benefits are less tangible. They include improved:

- reputation for being 'good to do business with';

- reputation for being ethical;

- reputation for social responsibility;

- customer/client retention and repeat business.

A RECOGNISED CHANGE PROGRAMME

It is essential that an implementation of stakeholder relationship management that introduces new processes and practices is treated as a change programme. It should be managed as any change programme is managed. Some suggestions for such a programme are:

- Ensure funding and resources are available.

- Get agreement for the objectives (success criteria) of the programme.

- Develop a plan with milestones and deliverables.

- Ensure engagement of the stakeholders of the change (perhaps using the methodology that is being implemented).

- Communicate frequently and regularly.

- Monitor the effectiveness of the communication (*step 4: engage; step 5: monitor*).

- Review progress and celebrate successes.

- Conduct a *lessons learned* review at the end of the programme and ensure that these learnings are added to the knowledge assets of the organisation.

Conclusion

The intention of this chapter has been to serve a number of purposes in assisting organisations to implement a stakeholder relationship management methodology, in particular the **Stakeholder** *Circle* methodology. The first purpose was to summarise the factors necessary for successful implementation of the methodology; the second was to provide the transition from using the **Stakeholder** *Circle* methodology for the success of one organisational activity to implementing the methodology as a universal tool for the organisation as a whole, or for significant parts of an organisation, such as a functional area or a division.

Chapters 8 and 9 will focus on the analysis, planning, implementation and review necessary for successful organisational implementation of a stakeholder relationship management methodology.

8

Defining Organisational Readiness

Chapter 7 summarised the issues an organisation needs to consider when it decides to implement systematic stakeholder relationship management to specific groups within the organisation or the organisation as a whole. This chapter discusses the choices open to management to implement the best or most appropriate processes based on the current capability of the organisation.

Successful implementation of stakeholder relationship management within an organisation requires consideration and application of the following factors: the effort of implementation must be aligned with the readiness of the organisation to absorb these new processes and practices – its *maturity* – and the implementation must be treated as a change programme. This chapter is organised to incorporate both of these essential factors: firstly, the concept of organisational maturity is discussed; this is then followed by a definition of the connection between organisational maturity and an organisation's readiness to implement a stakeholder relationship management methodology universally rather than just activity by activity. Stakeholder Relationship Management Maturity (SRMM) is introduced and guidelines developed for its use. The intention of these guidelines is to enable an organisation to successfully implement the most appropriate processes and practices of a stakeholder relationship management methodology – specifically the **Stakeholder** *Circle* methodology. Finally, examples are provided of organisations that illustrate the maturity levels.

Organisational Maturity Defined

Maturity is defined as being 'fully developed', or 'experienced, reliable, sensible'.[1] The concept of organisational maturity has been developed as a way for organisations to measure their performance in particular areas of their

---

1   http://www.merriam-webster.com/dictionary

business functionality and assess their existing practices against standards or benchmarks. A maturity model therefore, is a framework that provides a structured approach:

- for an organisation to assess its maturity;

- to establish a programme for improvement that moves from the existing level to a more advanced level.

Maturity models have been developed in many disciplines including risk management, IT software engineering, and project management. Some of the best known maturity models are:

- Risk Maturity Model developed by Hillson (1997);

- Capability Maturity Model Integration (CMMI) (Carnegie Mellon Institute 2006) developed for organisations to assess the maturity of and improve their software engineering processes and practices;

- Organizational Project Management Maturity Model – OPM3 (Project Management Institute 2008), to assist organisations that use projects to deliver business strategy.

The benefit to an organisation using a maturity model approach is that the structure enables the organisation to:

- define a starting point for their improvement efforts;

- create a common language and a shared vision within the boundaries of the maturity model;

- simplify approximations of reality to provide insight into the culture and processes within an organisation (Software Engineering Institute 2006).

To better understand how the benefits relate to organisational situations, a brief description of three well-known maturity models follows.

RISK MATURITY MODEL (RMM)

The Risk Maturity Model (RMM) describes four levels of maturity:

- Naïve (ad hoc): unaware of the need for risk management and operates in reactive mode if events occur that might have been predicted;

- Novice (initial): aware of the potential benefits of managing risk, no effectively implemented risk management processes;

- Normalised (repeatable): consistent processes for managing risk are used in most areas of the organisation, and benefits universally understood;

- Natural (managed): exhibits a risk-aware culture and a proactive approach to managing risk and opportunity.

Assessments for the RMM are based on how the organisation's risk management processes and practices fit the categories of:

- Culture: what is the level of awareness and acceptance of these processes and practices?

- Process: do formal processes exist: if so to what extent are they understood and complied with?

- Experience: how widespread is the understanding and use of language or concepts of these processes and practices?

- Application: to what extent are tools and techniques or dedicated resources available to assist in application of the processes and practices?

CAPABILITY MATURITY MODEL INTEGRATION (CMMI)

The Capability Maturity Model Integration (CMMI) from the Software Engineering Institute is perhaps the best known model of staged views of organisational maturity.[2]

---

2   Recently CMMI assessments have included the option of being carried out as continuous representations (Carnegie Mellon Institute 2006).

The five levels of CMMI maturity are usually described as:

- Initial (level 1): work is done in a reactive way; there is no consistent use of any agreed set of processes or practices.

- Managed (level 2): processes and practices may be used in discrete activities of an organisation: the selection of processes and practices will be the domain of the manager of that activity.

- Defined (level 3): processes and practices are develop by the organisation: proactive use of this common set of processes and practices is widespread.

- Quantitatively managed (level 4): the organisation measures the use of, and benefits realised from, the processes and practices;

- Optimising (level 5): focus on continuous improvement in the use of these processes and practices.

ORGANIZATIONAL PROJECT MANAGEMENT MATURITY MODEL (OPM3)

OPM3 is based on the concept that successful organisations will focus on delivering corporate strategy through projects (Project Management Institute 2008). The key to this strategy is therefore improvement in project management capability throughout the organisation – in projects, programs and portfolios. OPM3 does not use the concept of stages or levels to measure and advertise improvement. Rather it has focused on measuring the degree to which an organisation's consistent use of project management processes and practices conforms to a best practice set of competencies and capabilities. Measurement of process improvement is through measures of improvements in conformance to the best practices along a continuum: conformance is measured by percentage of conformance to pre-defined best practices. Within the OPM3 framework, continuous improvement in the form of a journey along the project management maturity path contributes to the achievement of organisational strategy through:

- doing the right projects: ensuring that projects and other organisational activities are funded and resourced in accordance with their capacity to deliver some aspect of the organisation's business strategy;

- doing the selected projects right: following a set of processes and practices as defined in the PMI project management standard, the *PMBOK Guide* (Project Management Institute 2008);

- applying the standard processes and practices consistently and across the organisation – time after time.

Readiness to Implement

Based on features of these maturity models, Stakeholder Relationship Management Maturity (SRMM) is proposed as a tool for measuring the levels of use of consistent, wide-spread stakeholder relationship management processes and practices. Each level of maturity described in SRMM defines the existing state of stakeholder relationship management in an organisation. This existing state is the starting point for planning the implementation of process improvements to enhance the effective management of stakeholder engagement within the organisation. In developing this concept, a number of levels of organisational readiness have been described that link:

- organisational willingness to engage proactively in developing and maintaining stakeholders relationships; and

- techniques, processes or practices that can assist in achieving those objectives.

Through an understanding of the level of readiness an organisation is closest to, its management can define the starting point for improvements in stakeholder relationship management. Using SRMM will enable effective and pragmatic implementation of stakeholder relationship management processes and practices within an organisation. It provides a framework for progressively building capability towards proactive and creative management of its stakeholder relationships in alignment with a structured approach to achieving organisational maturity in stakeholder relationship management.

The SRMM process model and guidelines for assessing and improving an organisation's stakeholder relationship management described in this chapter and the next, are based on the *steps* of the **Stakeholder** *Circle* methodology. However it is important to note that SRMM is independent of any particular methodology; the only requirement for effective use of SRMM is the adoption of a structured series of processes (repeatable and measurable) that can be built into the methodology chosen by an organisation.

COMPONENTS OF SUCCESSFUL STAKEHOLDER RELATIONSHIP MANAGEMENT

Development of descriptions of each level of the model is focused on how closely an organisation's current stakeholder relationship management processes and practices satisfy six different attributes (see Table 8.1)

Table 8.1   Attributes of stakeholder relationship management

Attribute	Description
Standard processes	Awareness and general use of standardised processes for stakeholder relationship management.
Centralised support	Centralised support for training, support and implementation of the standard processes and practices of stakeholder relationship management.
Improvements in stakeholder relationship management as part of KPIs	Organisation-wide implementation of stakeholder relationship management, and adoption as part of the organisational culture as the tool to manage and improve stakeholder relationship management in a specific activity area such as corporate social responsibility (CSR) or projects. The inclusion of measures of successful improvement in essential stakeholder relationships in management KPIs is a reliable indicator of adoption and use, as well as a useful motivation for its acceptance.
Organisation-wide implementation	Application of stakeholder relationship management processes and practices across a wide range of organisational activities including projects, programmes, competitor analysis and management, marketing strategies, CSR activities.
Developing baselines	Development of a typical view of a normal stakeholder community for each project type. Through the use, documentation and storage of graphical displays of characteristics of the stakeholder community in *step 3: visualise*, a view of a normal assembly of stakeholders (groups and individual roles), their relative importance and influence over the activity can be produced. This assembly will be the 'baseline', or standard for that type of activity within that organisational culture. This baseline will act as the point of comparison for stakeholder communities of new activities: conformance to this baseline indicates that there is less likely to be difficult stakeholders or lack of conformance in relationship management situations indicates that further analysis will be required to understand the reason for any anomalies.
Proactive reporting on stakeholder relationship management	Proactive use of the typical view of a stakeholder community (compared to a specific activity) for health reviews, risk assessment or other reviews. The use of a specific view of an organisation's typical community can contribute to an overall representation of progress and achievement of the objectives of specific organisational activities or of the effort of different parts of an organisation.

Stakeholder Relationship Management Maturity (SRMM)

Table 8.2 summarises the five levels if SRMM. Each level is described in more detail in Tables 8.3 to 8.7 below. Description of each level will be further enhanced by examples of typical organisations that will have been assessed at specific levels of maturity.

The five levels of SRMM are:

- Level 1 – Ad hoc: some use of processes, but isolated, reactive and not consistent;

- Level 2 – Procedural: focus on processes and tools, as a reflection of focus on delivering traditional, measurable results – schedule, budget and quality, without necessarily recognising the importance of relationships with stakeholders;

Table 8.2   Summary of criteria of SRMM levels

SRMM Levels	Standard processes	Central support	Org-wide use within an activity type	Beyond single activity type	Typical stakeholder communities	Risk handling & health reviews
1. Ad hoc: some use of processes	Some	No	No	No	No	No
2. Procedural: focus on processes and tools	Yes	Some	No	Some	No	No
3. Relational: focus on the stakeholders and mutual benefits	Yes	Yes	Some	Some	Some	No
4. Integrated: methodology repeatable, integrated	Yes	Yes	Yes	Some	Some	Some
5. Predictive: health checks and other predictive assessments	Yes	Yes	Yes	Yes	Yes	Yes

- Level 3 – Relational: focus on the stakeholders and mutual benefits, and the recognition that communication is the tool for stakeholder relationship management, but the communication must be targeted to meet the needs (often conflicting) of the stakeholder community as well as the needs of the organisation, but within the capacity and capability of the team;

- Level 4 – Integrated: the organisation's methodology is repeatable and integrated across all areas and functions of the organisation that are responsible for activities that in some way contribute to the organisation's business strategy;

- Level 5 – Predictive: used for health checks and predictive risk assessment and other creative and proactive ways to measure improvements in the delivery of the business' strategy.

LEVEL 1: AD HOC

This level is characterised by isolated pockets of awareness of the need for stakeholder management and through the use of simple tools; see Table 8.3.

Table 8.3   Level 1 defined

Maturity Category	Exists?	Comments
Standardised Processes.	Some	Isolated attempts to use various stakeholder management methodologies.
Centralised Support.	No	Support, where it exists, is through personal networks.
Organisation-wide implementation for a type of activity: stakeholder relationship management is part of KPIs.	No	Some relationship management 'heroes'; but the implementation is usually confined to the arena of influence of that individual. The relationship usually fragments when the 'hero' moves to another role or leaves the organisation.
Application beyond a single activity type or area.	No	Stakeholder relationship management processes and practices are usually only focused on a few projects or specific problems.
Development of a typical view of a normal stakeholder community.	No	Where used, stakeholder data and communication plans are developed in isolation during a planning phase and rarely updated.
Proactive use of the typical view of a normal stakeholder community for risk assessment, health reviews.	No	Any health reviews are conducted as a reaction to the potential failure of a high-profile activity. No concept of regular reviews as a part of continuous improvement exists.

LEVEL 2: PROCEDURAL

This level (see Table 8.4) is characterised by:

- some individuals having knowledge of the importance of stakeholder relationship management;

- routine use of tools and processes in a single or isolated activity area;

- an internal focus on measurement of the benefits – schedule, budget and scope management of these activities.

Table 8.4   Level 2 defined

Maturity Category	Exists?	Comments
Standardised Processes.	Yes	But processes not widely accepted or used. Organisation focus is on rolling out standard tools and processes.
Centralised Support.	Some	Support exists through manuals, supplier support mechanisms, or local experts.
Organisation-wide implementation for a type of activity; stakeholder relationship management is part of KPIs.	No	Some relationship management 'heroes' still exist within the organisation. Process or tools may generate stakeholder relationship management reports that can be included, either whole or in summary, for reporting where used.
Application beyond a single activity type or area.	Some	Limited recognition of the need to focus on stakeholder relationship management beyond projects: for programmes or organisation-specific needs such as pre-qualification of tender bids.
Development of a typical view of a normal stakeholder community.	No	The value of tracking and updating information on each project's unique community is recognised but not integrated across the organisation.
Proactive use of the typical view of a normal stakeholder community for risk assessment, health reviews.	No	Any health reviews are conducted as a reaction to the potential failure of a high-profile activity. No concept of regular reviews as a part of continuous improvement exists.

LEVEL 3: RELATIONAL

This level (see Table 8.5) is characterised by:

- more generalised understanding of the importance of stakeholder relationship management;

- an external focus on engaging stakeholders;

- use of tools and processes to achieve and measure improvements in stakeholder relationship management across an expanding range of activities;

- a specific focus on mutual benefits, with communication targeted to meet the expectations and requirements of important stakeholders as well as the needs of the activity.

Table 8.5   Level 3 defined

Maturity Category	Exists?	Comments
Standardised Processes.	Yes	The use of a standard methodology is recognised and expected. Effective stakeholder management is seen as important in the successful delivery of business initiatives and projects. Managers focus on mutuality and shared benefits.
Centralised Support.	Yes	A Centre of Excellence (or similar) provides some formal support, mentoring and training.
Organisation-wide implementation for a type of activity; stakeholder relationship management part of KPIs.	Some	The use of stakeholder relationship management starts to expand beyond a single activity type or area. Some aspects of stakeholder relationship management are included in some managers' KPIs. Information, data and graphical reporting formats showing changes/improvements in stakeholder attitudes used to guide some decision-making.
Application beyond a single activity type or area.	Some	The recognition of the benefit of application of stakeholder relationship management processes and practices for applications such as mergers and acquisitions, bid preparation analysis, project and programme management, competitor analysis and management spreads.
Development of a typical view of a normal stakeholder community.	Some	There is recognition of the need to maintain updated data on each stakeholder community; standardised processes and tools support this and incorporate the means to illustrate the community in an organisation-specific manner. Spreadsheets or multi-dimension graphical representation becomes important.
Proactive use of the typical view of a normal stakeholder community for risk assessment, health reviews.	No	Any health reviews are conducted as a reaction to the potential failure of a high-profile activity. No concept of regular reviews as a part of continuous improvement exists.

LEVEL 4: INTEGRATED

This level (see Table 8.6) is characterised by:

- commitment to continuous improvement;

- strong internal support for this commitment within the organisation;

- recognition that individual stakeholders may be involved in many activities and may transfer support or opposition from one to another if expectations are met, or not met;

- more organisational personnel gaining experience in using stakeholder relationship management processes and practices successfully;

- use of tools and processes to integrate information and gain insight;

Table 8.6   Level 4 defined

Maturity Category	Exists?	Comments
Standardised Processes.	Yes	The organisation's focus moves to measuring the practical benefits of effective stakeholder engagement and management.
Centralised Support.	Yes	Central Support Unit dedicated to stakeholder relationship management training, support and mentoring.
Organisation-wide implementation for a type of activity; stakeholder relationship management part of KPIs.	Yes	Stakeholder relationship management is included in key managers' KPIs. Information, data and graphical reporting formats showing changes/improvements in stakeholder attitudes used to guide some decision-making.
Application beyond a single activity type or area.	Some	The development of specific applications to meet the organisation's unique needs may occur to facilitate the development of specific communication strategies and plans.
Development of a typical view of a normal stakeholder community.	Some	Standardised data allows analysis of stakeholder issues, opportunities and threats on an ad hoc basis.
Proactive use of the typical view of a normal stakeholder community for risk assessment, health reviews.	Some	The assessment of the stakeholder community is a routine part of the organisation's assessment of risk, opportunities, successful delivery of the outcomes of activities.

- recognition of overall benefits of using stakeholder relationship management processes and practices for managing diverse and conflicting stakeholder expectations to achieve win–win for stakeholders and the activity.

LEVEL 5: PREDICTIVE

This level (see Table 8.7) is characterised by:

- corporate management focus with collection of *lessons learned* (historical) data in a knowledge management system;

- regular use of data about the stakeholder community for health checks on the progress of the activity (does the data conform to 'normal'?);

Table 8.7   Level 5 defined

Maturity Category	Exists?	Comments
Standardised Processes.	Yes	The organisation's focus moves to measuring the practical benefits of effective stakeholder engagement and management.
Centralised Support.	Yes	Central Support Unit dedicated to stakeholder relationship management training, support and mentoring.
Organisation-wide implementation for a type of activity; stakeholder relationship management part of KPIs.	Yes	Stakeholder relationship management is included in key managers' KPIs. Information, data and graphical reporting formats showing changes/improvements in stakeholder attitudes used to guide some decision-making.
Application beyond a single activity type or area.	Yes	The development of specific applications to meet the organisation's unique needs occurs as part of the process to facilitate the development of specific communication strategies and plans.
Development of a typical view of a normal stakeholder community.	Yes	Standardised data allows analysis of stakeholder issues, opportunities and threats as part of the regular reporting package.
Proactive use of the typical view of a normal stakeholder community for risk assessment, health reviews.	Yes	The assessment of stakeholders is a routine part of the organisation's assessment of risk, opportunities, etc. Graphical reporting on aspects of the stakeholder community are an essential part of the reporting package.

- predictive risk assessment: using historical data, the experience of the team, an understanding of the stakeholder community, in particular which stakeholders require more attention, because they are not as engaged as is necessary for success of the activity;

- a commitment to improved corporate social responsibility (CSR) as part of the organisation's mission and vision.

Examples of SRMM Levels

TYPICAL ORGANISATIONAL STRUCTURES OR ENVIRONMENTS FOR EACH STAGE

The idea and the data that forms the SRMM categories have originated from experiences in working with organisations to implement the *Stakeholder Circle* methodology and in some cases the *Stakeholder Circle* software tool. This next section describes the organisations that formed the basis for these SRMM categorisations.

Level 1: Major European transport company

This organisation was a division of a global transport company, operating in an increasingly competitive market. All opportunities for expansion within the industry were hard fought because of the emergence of intense competition from a number of transport companies newly entering the field. Management recognised that developing a culture of stakeholder relationship management within the organisation would be a winning strategy. The state of stakeholder relationship management in the company before the implementation of the *Stakeholder Circle* methodology was ad hoc and reactive. One particular group in the division led the initiative, beginning with a series of training workshops.

Although awareness and use of any stakeholder relationship management in the organisation was almost non-existent, management was keen to support the implementation of the methodology and incorporated some sophisticated methods to ensure its acceptance by all personnel within the organisation. They conveyed strong messages of commitment to the success of the programme through:

- introducing each training course and emphasising the importance of the methodology;

- attending the course;

- featuring the programme in several editions of their in-house magazine;

- including introduction of the programme and clear measures of success in the KPIs of management of each of their regions.

Level 2: Australian state government department #1

The exemplar for level 2 was a programme group within a state government department. The group had been directed to do a CMMI assessment. The results of the assessment showed, among other things, that there was a need for the implementation of standard tools and processes to support stakeholder relationship management. The *Stakeholder Circle* software tool was introduced within the group. The first project it was applied to was a complex, high profile, politically sensitive programme. The team spent two days applying the methodology supported by the tool and identified over 100 stakeholders. The programme itself, but also the use of the software tool to support the programme, was supported by senior management to the extent that they attended the stakeholder analysis workshops contributing their knowledge of the political and cultural relationships that would affect the success of the programme. The communication plan was established and a communication schedule developed and published. However, the communication plan was never updated, the team claiming that they were 'too busy' on the tactical issues surrounding completion of the programme.

The programme group initiating the introduction and application of the methodology aspired to improve their stakeholder relationship management and achieve their goal of continuous improvement. However, the organisation did not put into place the necessary infrastructure to support the team longer-term. The maintenance of a current view of the right stakeholders and a current communication plan was impossible for the team without the necessary strategic support. The team members were simply overwhelmed with the day-to-day tactical work of managing such a complex, politically sensitive programme.

Table 8.8   Summary of level 2 organisation

Description	Level 2 organisation components
Senior management support	Total involvement and support
Standard processes and practices implemented	Attention paid to good planning and documentation
Plans and documentation	'Too busy' for maintenance of plans and documentation
Long-term central support	Not implemented

Level 3: Major European transport company – post implementation

The implementation of the *Stakeholder Circle* methodology resulted in the organisation described as being at level 1 re-assessed at level 3 after a year of implementation effort. The management of the division decided not to implement the *Stakeholder Circle* database, and developed an in-house spreadsheet-based tool that was better suited to the organisation's culture. It was sufficient to provide an appropriate level of reporting on stakeholder relationship management activities within the core responsibilities of that division. At the time of writing, the methodology is now considered as a part of the toolkit for personnel fulfilling their duties within the environment of the organisation. The outcome of the culture change based on stakeholder relationship management is recognition that building and maintaining stakeholder relationships are just as important for the success of their activities as managing financial aspects of the business.

Table 8.9   Summary of level 3 organisation

Description	Level 3 organisation components
Senior management support	Total involvement and support
Standard processes and practices implemented	Tool developed Training programme delivered organisation-wide
Plans and documentation	Available from central web-site
Long-term central support	Central expertise provided

Level 4: Australian state government department #2

A growing environmental protection (climate change) attitude is leading the movement away from uncontrolled use of private vehicles to development of strategies for co-ordinated and more efficient networks of public transport within the state boundaries. The sponsor of the group developing the strategy realised that management of the conflicting and diverse needs and requirements of the groups and individuals impacted was essential for success of this initiative. Plans for commissioning the strategy and developing recommendations for implementation included understanding who were the important stakeholders and how best to engage them. The *Stakeholder Circle* methodology and database were adopted. Multiple consultations were used to identify stakeholders at all levels within the structure of the region. This organisation demonstrated level 4 readiness to implement the *Stakeholder Circle,* even proposing a creative additional use of the methodology and software to provide the ability to develop programme reports for each level of consultations planned throughout the region.

Table 8.10   Summary of level 4 organisation

Description	Level 4 organisation components
Senior management support	Total involvement and support
Standard processes and practices implemented	Tool developed Training programme delivered organisation-wide
Plans and documentation	Available from central web-site
Long-term central support	Central expertise provided

Level 5: Australian federal government department

An initiative was begun in an Australian federal government department to develop a series of reports for regular reviews of large complex projects as part of their continuous improvement plan for the department. Projects undertaken by this department were complex, with a timeline of many years. The projects were impacted by political issues and interference from high-ranking government officials. The review process consisted of developing benchmark reports showing both project team members and management alike what a healthy project in this culture and at this stage would look like. Reviews would consist of comparing the baseline with the current data and attempting to reconcile or explain any differences. From a stakeholder relationship management and communication perspective, baselines would be developed from a series of a stakeholder analyses on the projects at each phase. Any fluctuations from the baseline depiction of the community within that organisational culture were to be analysed and necessary remediation conducted before issues became urgent and threatened the successful delivery of the project objectives.

Table 8.11   Summary of level 5 organisation

Description	Level 5 organisation components
Senior management support	Total involvement and support
Standard processes and practices implemented	Tool developed Training programme delivered organisation-wide
Plans and documentation	Available from central web-site
Long-term central support	Central expertise provided Mentoring and coaching Baselines developed

Conclusion

Stakeholder Relationship Management Maturity (SRMM) has been developed as a measure of the readiness of an organisation to introduce stakeholder relationship management process and practices. It is primarily a tool for organisations. SRMM can be of significant benefit when used to support the development of stakeholder management within a project. However, it will be of greater benefit when applied to all organisational activities (project and operational) in a staged approach, supported by a well-constructed methodology and tool-set such as the *Stakeholder* Circle.

Developing a full capability of stakeholder relationship management within an organisation is a costly exercise for an organisation. The introduction and implementation of a staged approach such as that identified in the SRMM model will increase the chance of success and assist the organisation in realising the objectives and benefits from the investment in its people and its processes.

Chapter 9 will focus on implementing the appropriate stakeholder relationship management process and practices through the use of elements of the *Stakeholder* Circle methodology.

9

Implementation Guidelines

Chapter 8 described the concept of different levels of readiness of an organisation to introduce new stakeholder relationship management processes and practices, or implement improvements to existing processes and practices. It described a set of characteristics for each level of stakeholder relationship management maturity to allow an organisation to gauge its current level. From that baseline the organisation can introduce additional processes and practices, or improve the awareness or the application of existing processes and practices in a structured and measurable manner. This chapter provides guidelines to support the organisation in this implementation. It is organised as follows: guidelines for moving from one level to another are described; approaches based on the model of the *Stakeholder Circle* methodology (described in Chapters 3–6) are recommended and essential components of change management are described.

Guidelines for Improvement

Whatever the catalyst for undertaking improvements in stakeholder relationship management, an organisational change is required along with tactics and strategies to encourage the cooperation or minimise the opposition of internal stakeholders. For the change to be successful, actions to ensure that the improvements are accepted by the stakeholders of the change must be factored into the improvement plan. To facilitate this, the organisation should consider a number of factors:

- The specific set of actions to implement the change are best managed as a project.

- The project must be appropriately:

    - funded;

- – resourced;

- – managed.

- • Managing this activity using the disciplines of project management includes managing the relationships within the activity's stakeholder community.

- • The team implementing stakeholder relationship management processes and practices must use and showcase the set of processes and practices it is planning to introduce into the organisation.

Achieving the Next Level

The *Stakeholder Circle* methodology and supporting tools are the basis of the guidelines discussed in this chapter. However it is important to note that application of the concepts of SRMM for implementation of stakeholder relationship management processes and practices is *independent of any particular methodology*. The only requirement for effective application of SRMM is the use of a structured series of processes (repeatable and measurable) that can be built into any methodology used by an organisation.

Guidelines for implementation are shown in Table 9.1.[1] For each SRMM level, the guidelines provide information on:

- • features of each level including descriptions of the characteristics of each level by a focus on:

- – culture;

- – experience;

- – process;

- – application[2] (Hillson 1997);

---

1 Table 9.1 is located at the end of this chapter.
2 This description set was first used to describe a Risk Maturity Model developed by Hillson (1997).

- suggestions on aspects of stakeholder relationship management methodology that would best match the current level of organisational readiness;

- suggestions for reporting procedures and types of tools that may assist the organisation in managing stakeholder relationships within the framework described;

- additional information that may assist the organisation in its implementation efforts.

ACHIEVING LEVEL 1: AD HOC

Level 1: ad hoc is the default position of many organisations. An organisation that is assessed at level 1 may not necessarily be financially failing or organisationally in disarray. It may:

- not need to be profitable:

    - a *not-for-profit* organisation;

    - a government body;

    - a division of a successful parent company.

- operate in a niche market;

- have long-term loyal customers;

- have stable and satisfactory stakeholder relationships.

Table 9.2   Level 1 features

SRMM Stages	Standard processes	Central support	Org-wide use within an activity type	Beyond a single activity type	Typical stakeholder communities	Risk handling & health reviews
1. Ad hoc: some use of processes	Some	No	No	No	No	No

Features

The features of a level 1 organisation's stakeholder relationship management processes and practices are shown in Tables 9.2 and 9.3,[3] previously described in detail in Chapter 8. The organisation may have previously adopted methodologies, processes and practices as part of its strategies for improvement in its functional areas. Personnel may be unaware or unwilling to follow the processes. Stakeholder relationship management is seen as a good thing, and often there are claims that personnel are 'managing stakeholders already'. This stakeholder management will usually be intuitive, irregular, exclusive to the individual or group and rarely consistent with the views and actions of others in the organisation doing similar work.

Best fit activities

Within a level 1 organisation, the most effective approach will be introducing small changes requiring minimal additional effort to generate immediate results. The most effective starting point is targeted communication[4] to important stakeholders: it is the key to a successful stakeholder relationship management effort. This can best be facilitated by introducing *step 4: engage* accompanied by *step 5: monitor*.[5] The simple graphic resulting from the application of these *steps* is easily added to regular progress reports and easily interpreted. Figure 9.1 shows output from application of these *steps*.

Benefits of using this approach will be:

- Generally the manager and/or the team will have a means to identify stakeholders and a view on who is most important. While this approach to understanding stakeholders may not be consistent or structured, a communication strategy based on these principles can identify important stakeholders and reduce potential resistance.

- The team will be introduced to the structure and the idea of working together[6] to understand their stakeholders better through use of

---

3   Please see Table 9.3 at end of this chapter.
4   Chapter 5 describes the processes of targeted communication.
5   Chapters 5 and 6 describe *step 4: engage* and *step 5: monitor.*
6   Chapter 3 defines the importance of the team to successful stakeholder relationship management.

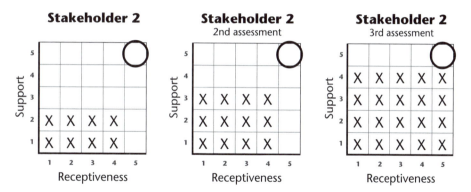

Figure 9.1 **Examples of level 1 implementation**

the five levels of *support* and *receptiveness* that together describe the *attitude* of the stakeholder.

- By using the targeted communication approach that results from the analysis described in Figure 9.1, the team will be able to better manage its scarce resources – time and people – through understanding where best to focus its efforts.

- The engagement profile shown in Figure 9.1 will give busy managers a clear picture of key aspects of the stakeholder community, and the results of the team's communication efforts over time.

- The engagement profile matrix is easily developed, understood and updated.

- Existing reports can be adapted or new engagement profile reports can be produced manually.

Types of reporting and tools

The tools that can support implementation of this simple approach may be:

- informal: MS Word documents or Excel spreadsheets;

- the organisation's existing methodology and reports;

- in-house: developed to provide data to support the implementation.

The engagement profile can readily form part of any set of tools and reports.

Additional information

The team may be initially enthusiastic about introducing new stakeholder relationship management processes and practices into their work. However, the enthusiasm may diminish as the daily requirements of the work cause energy, time and resources to be diverted into dealing with tactical issues. To maintain impetus, senior managers must support this early implementation through practical involvement and incentives.

FROM LEVEL 1 TO LEVEL 2: PROCEDURAL

The triggers for organisations seeking to improve stakeholder relationship management may include:

- a requirement for more efficiency as part of:

  - a government initiative;

  - a requirement by the parent company for more autonomous operations;

  - a new era of open competition;

  - niche products maturing and being replaced by more modern products or services.

Implementation of new processes and practices means new ways of doing things. It is important to:

- take small steps: moving from any *level* to an improved *level* cannot be hurried;

- have a clear plan for this programme of improvement in stakeholder relationship management in the organisation;

- ensure that the objectives are clearly defined; and

- define critical success factors to confirm the next *level* has been reached before considering moving to a higher level (one step at a time!).

Table 9.4   Level 2 features

SRMM Stages	Standard processes	Central support	Org-wide use within an activity type	Beyond a single activity type	Typical stakeholder communities	Risk handling & health reviews
2. Procedural: focus on processes and tools	Yes	Some	No	Some	No	No

Features of level 2

The existing methodologies that the organisation may have endorsed are being re-affirmed, replaced or updated, and a stronger focus is placed on stakeholder relationship management: see Table 9.5.[7]

Best fit activities

Having embraced *steps 4 and 5,* the organisation should retrofit aspects of the other *steps* of the **Stakeholder** *Circle* methodology, especially recognition that:

- collection of information about stakeholders early in the planning of the activity is essential to support more effective communication;

- subjectivity can be minimised by using a structured, repeatable approach to understanding who is important.

Types of reporting and tools

Additional tools should support recognition of the importance of:

- gathering information;

---

7   Table 9.5 can be found at the of this chapter.

- maintaining a history or audit trail (to measure effective communication); and

- reporting on progress and issues associated with managing the stakeholder relationships.

These tools should be in the form of:

- MS Word templates and work instructions (to support a consistent approach);

- spreadsheets with macros for calculations, sorting and other more sophisticated operations;

- a simple database to provide additional capability to store and retrieve data for comparisons as well as provision of simple graphics.

The *stakeholder-on-a-page* (SOAP) is a preformatted MS Word template designed to record stakeholder information and allow three updates of assessments of an activity's stakeholder community.[8] The example of the SOAP template is shown in Figure 9.2 opposite.

An example of an in-house report that may be developed by the organisation using data gathering by the team in following the *steps* of the **Stakeholder** *Circle* methodology is shown in Figure 9.3 on page 182.

Additional information

Examples of triggers for moving from an ad hoc *level* of stakeholder relationship management process and practice are listed in the early part of this section. It is therefore reasonable to expect that management will offer more encouragement and incentive for this move from *ad hoc* to *procedural*. As with any major change, the involvement, encouragement and commitment of the leadership team is critical.

---

8   Chapter 4 describes these tools and their uses for stakeholder relationship management.

Stakeholder *Management* Pty Ltd

stakeholder-on-a-page

Stakeholder Name _____

Directions of Influence: U__D__O__S__ and I__E__

Stake		
I __	R __
O __	N __
I __	C __

Requires from the work: _____

Importance to the work: _____

Prioritise the Stakeholder

Assessment	Power Rate 1 - 4	Proximity Rate 1 - 4	Value Rate 1 - 5	Action Rate 1 - 5	Index # / Priority #

Build Engagement Profile (see note)

First assessment — Support (5,4,3,2,1) vs Receptiveness (1,2,3,4,5)

Next assessment — Support (5,4,3,2,1) vs Receptiveness (1,2,3,4,5)

Next assessment — Support (5,4,3,2,1) vs Receptiveness (1,2,3,4,5)

Use **X** when assessing the current engagement profile of each stakeholder and **O** to indicate the optimal engagement profile

*Influence on?*_____ *Influenced by?*_____

Communication Plan

Message	Messenger	Format (W/O F/I)	Frequency	Assessment date	Comments

Relationship Manager: owns the relationship _____

Figure 9.2   SOAP template

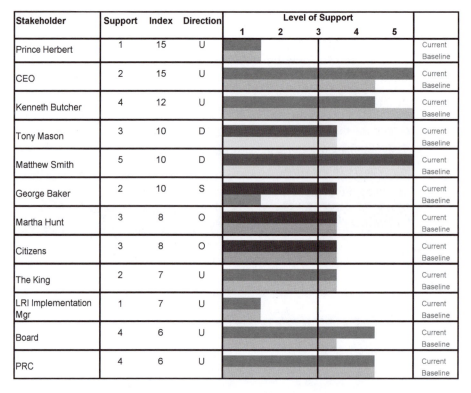

Stakeholder	Support	Index	Direction	Level of Support					
				1	2	3	4	5	
Prince Herbert	1	15	U						Current Baseline
CEO	2	15	U						Current Baseline
Kenneth Butcher	4	12	U						Current Baseline
Tony Mason	3	10	D						Current Baseline
Matthew Smith	5	10	D						Current Baseline
George Baker	2	10	S						Current Baseline
Martha Hunt	3	8	O						Current Baseline
Citizens	3	8	O						Current Baseline
The King	2	7	U						Current Baseline
LRI Implementation Mgr	1	7	U						Current Baseline
Board	4	6	U						Current Baseline
PRC	4	6	U						Current Baseline

Figure 9.3   In-house report

FROM LEVEL 2 TO LEVEL 3: RELATIONAL

The impetus for an even stronger focus on stakeholder relationship management may be the result of management initiatives such as:

- new leadership team defining new ways to:

  - achieve efficiency (reduce costs);

  - increase output (of goods or services).

- management deciding to undergo productivity improvements and:

  - assessing its current state;

  - identifying new processes and procedures to achieve improvement;

- agreeing that stakeholder relationship management will be included in any improvement programmes.

- management deciding to improve stakeholder relationship management in a specific division, or specific programmes and seeing the benefits of views of interrelationships with other work;

- a shift in emphasis on new business strategies (and more effective means to achieve them) because of changes in the market or industry;

- recognising that changes in the market may require new creative approaches to:

  - competitor analysis and management;

  - partner analysis and management.

Features

The move to level 3: relational is often marked by the need to focus on a particular business strategy such as competitor analysis, partner management or a change such as a merger with another company or acquisition of another company. The focus is on mutual benefits or at least understanding the diverse cultures and expectations of the other parties. The features of this *level* are summarised in Table 9.6 and key characteristics in Table 9.7.[9]

Best fit activities

The teams managing the events on behalf of the organisation should use all five *steps* of the **Stakeholder** *Circle* methodology. Benefits of using this approach are:

- The events or situations that have triggered this requirement for improved and consistent stakeholder relationship management processes and practices require focused remedies or solutions.

- The organisation may not have encountered such situations before; a proven methodology will assist in achieving the best possible outcomes.

---

9   Table 9.7 can be found at the end of this chapter.

Table 9.6   Level 3 features

SRMM Stages	Standard processes	Central support	Org-wide use within an activity type	Beyond a single activity type	Typical stakeholder communities	Risk handling & health reviews
3. Relational: focus on the stakeholders and mutual benefits	Yes	Yes	Some	Some	Some	No

Types of reporting and tools

The tools and reports designed to support the *Stakeholder* *Circle* methodology should be used to best effect. These tools can be:

- produced by the various *Stakeholder* *Circle* methodology tools, such as SOAP, SWS or SIMS;[10]

- developed by the organisation to produce the necessary data, but within the standard reporting software adopted by the organisation.

Figure 9.4 provides an example of how an organisation at level 3 may use data from their stakeholder relationship management processes and practices as management reporting and evidence of progress. These reports can show evidence of improvement in *attitude* of specific important stakeholders through simple purpose-built reports based on data gathered in *steps 1 and 2*.

This report structure has the benefit of having a similar format to the '2x2 matrix' structure described in Chapter 4. It uses the prioritised stakeholder information and combines it with measure of *support* to indicate important stakeholders whose levels of engagement need to be improved. Report #2 shows that the *support* of their important stakeholders has been improved but in the process of focusing on some stakeholders others may feel neglected and exhibit lower levels of *support* at the next review. Is the bonus granted for improving the *support* level of stakeholder 1 and stakeholder 11, or are there penalties for the reduction in *support* of stakeholder 5 and 7? Answering these questions

---

10 Chapter 4 describes tools to assist in the storage and retrieval of stakeholder relationship management information.

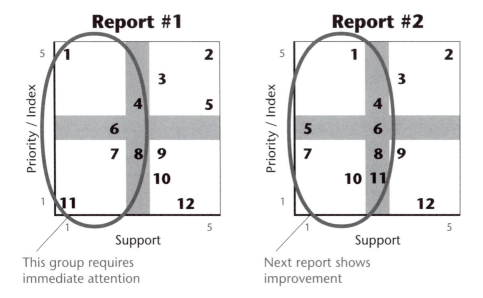

Figure 9.4   Example of management reporting

satisfactorily is tied to appropriate communication between the individual and management and the setting of measurement criteria – all these aspects are part of the focus and practice of stakeholder relationship management applied to staff and HR practices.

Additional information

Since this application of the *Stakeholder Circle* methodology is in support of specific events or situations, there may not be any focus on continuous improvement of processes and practices. The central support unit that has been introduced to support the level 3 activities should also have as its charter communication strategies to spread the news about the benefits of the level 3 approaches. It should also begin to develop a campaign to raise the profile of their work, and encourage the organisation to attain level 4 at the appropriate time.

FROM LEVEL 3 TO LEVEL 4: INTEGRATED

The success of level 3 processes and practices, along with the acceptance of the need to better manage stakeholder relationships across all of the organisation's activities, means that the organisation will begin to adopt all aspects of stakeholder relationship management processes and practices as part of business-as-usual practices.

Features

Because there is a natural progression there should be little resistance to the incorporation of stakeholder relationship management in all the organisation's activities. The benefits of this consistent approach will be recognised by all. The features of this level are summarised in Table 9.8 above and key characteristics in Table 9.9.[11]

Table 9.8   Level 4 features

SRMM Stages	Standard processes	Central support	Org-wide use within an activity type	Beyond a single activity type	Typical stakeholder communities	Risk handling & health reviews
4. Integrated: methodology repeatable, integrated	Yes	Yes	Yes	Some	Some	Some

Best fit activities

All *steps* are relevant to the task of stakeholder relationship management.

Types of reporting and tools

The tools and reports designed to support the **Stakeholder** *Circle* methodology will be embraced to best effect. These tools can be:

- produced by the various items of **Stakeholder** *Circle* methodology software, such as SOAP, SWS or SIMS;[12]

- developed by the organisation to produce the necessary data, but within the standard reporting software adopted by the organisation.

An example of more sophisticated reporting enabled by consistent collection of data and using it for monitoring and measuring progress is the overall engagement matrix – an output of SIMS, see Figure 9.5.

---

11 Table 9.9 can be found at the end of this chapter.
12 Chapter 4 describes tools to support stakeholder relationship management activities.

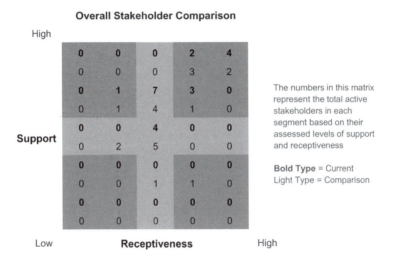

Overall Stakeholder Engagement Index

	Index	Version	
Current	**69.495**	3	22/12/2008
Previous	61.598	1	23/04/2008
Trend	**Some Improvement**		

The 'index' value is the aggregate weighting of all stakeholders on a scale of 0 to 100.

Overall Stakeholder Comparison

The numbers in this matrix represent the total active stakeholders in each segment based on their assessed levels of support and receptiveness

Bold Type = Current
Light Type = Comparison

Figure 9.5   Overall Engagement Index

The overall engagement index

The primary purpose of engaging in stakeholder relationship management is to:

- minimise the threats to the activity's success caused by antagonistic stakeholders;

- maximise the opportunities for success by:

  – building understanding;

  – managing stakeholder expectations;

  – managing perceptions of the important stakeholders.

As the work of the activity proceeds and the team implements its communication strategy and ensures that it understands which stakeholders are important, it is reasonable to expect a general improvement in the *attitude* of the entire stakeholder community towards the activity.

The overall engagement index produced from data entered into the **Stakeholder** *Circle* database (SIMS) provides a high level summary of the *attitude* of the current stakeholder community compared to the summary of *attitude* recorded at an earlier time in the activity. While Figure 9.5 shows a desirable, general improvement, it is important to recognise that this report is only useful in a general way to show overall progress. However, it gives no detailed view of issues that may need to be managed with individual key stakeholders. Important stakeholders need to be reviewed individually. The value of this is a record or report showing whether or not the overall community of stakeholders is responding favourably to relationship management efforts of the team.

SIMS

Full use of the features of SIMS will benefit the organisation in retaining level 4.

The screen dump of a stakeholder information page in Figure 9.6 shows how the information obtained from *steps 1–4* can be displayed. SIMS also has the capability of retaining previous iterations of the data collected, so a full audit trail is available, as well as the essential graphics for monitoring trends including:

- the **Stakeholder** *Circle* depiction of the stakeholder community at each stage;

- the previous and current engagement profile for each stakeholder;

- the overall engagement matrix for *attitudes* of all important stakeholders of the activity.

Additional information

The **Stakeholder** *Circle* methodology, its tools and reports are used as a demonstration of repeatable application within the organisation.

FROM LEVEL 4 TO LEVEL 5: PREDICTIVE

The only example I have encountered of an organisation at this level was restricted to a single government department, and only for a short time. That

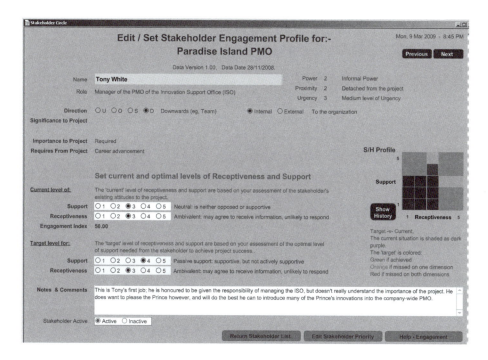

Figure 9.6   Screen dump of a stakeholder page from SIMS

organisation is described in Chapter 8. The achievement of level 5 features was the result of two factors:

- Management decisions to improve the delivery of very long and high-cost projects through strategies to increase levels of:

    – support;

    – control; and

    – mentoring provided by the central support unit.

- The appointment of a new manager to ensure these requirements were delivered. She implemented:

    – a mentoring programme, where experienced PM were trained to coach the less experienced;

    – a series of baselines defined as the acceptable model for all aspects of management of projects, including the use of the

Stakeholder Circle as the template for stakeholder management practices;

– a system of regular health reviews of all projects;

– urgent action plans for those projects that did not meet the set criteria.

Table 9.10   Level 5 features

SRMM Stages	Standard processes	Central support	Org-wide use within an activity type	Beyond a single activity type	Typical stakeholder communities	Risk handling & health reviews
5. Predictive: health checks and other predictive assessments	Yes	Yes	Yes	Yes	Yes	Yes

Features

A level 5 organisation will have a consistent set of processes and practices as part of the way things are done. At regular health reviews, reports of progress and issues within each of the activities will be compared to the baseline, and the results used for acknowledgement that further investigation is necessary, or remedial actions required or to provide positive evidence of success or progress (Table 9.11 summarises characteristics).[13]

Best fit activities

The **Stakeholder** Circle methodology has been accepted in full for stakeholder relationship management. Software has been introduced to assist, particularly in monitoring of communication effectiveness and trend analysis.

Types of reporting and tools

Each team is encouraged to select the type of software support tools that best meet their needs, whether SOAP, SWS or SIMS.

---

13 Table 9.11 can be found at the end of this chapter.

An essential report will be the **Stakeholder** *Circle* map of the current stakeholder community. This should be compared to the baseline developed from the organisation and type of activity for early detection of anomalies. The anomalies may show negative properties of key or important stakeholders – a trigger for further analysis and investigations.[14]

Additional information

This information can be used in many ways, including:

- promotion of the organisation's intention for the outcomes of an activity;

- raising the profile of the activity or the profile of the organisation;

- gaining more attention for the execution or outcomes of the activity;

- announcing the membership of the stakeholder community to increase the commitment of the community's members for the activity.

The information may also prove valuable in understanding the perceptions, fears and objections of stakeholders opposed to the activity to help mitigate or at least manage the opposition.

FACTORS FOR SUCCESSFUL ORGANISATIONAL IMPLEMENTATION

Successful implementation of any change requires attention to the following:

- how the change is planned, resourced and implemented using project management disciplines;

- understanding and managing uncertainty and resistance;

- obtaining support for the change programme;

- following the three phases of a successful change;

- measuring and celebrating success.

---

14 These maps are shown in chapter 4 as outputs from SIMS.

Using project management disciplines

To ensure the change programme has a greater chance of success, the application of project management tools, techniques and disciplines is recommended. A project that is established, resourced and managed appropriately will have the following features:

- approved funds;

- committed resources;

- dedicated project manager assigned;

- committed sponsor designated;

- appropriate reporting mechanisms in place to monitor:

  - progress;

  - issue and risk.

- stakeholder community identified:

  - right stakeholders;

  - key and important stakeholders;

  - targeted communication;

  - effectiveness measures.

Considerations for managing uncertainty

At each of the levels of organisational maturity, integration of the processes and practices into the culture of the organisation is essential. The effort of implementing the improvements to stakeholder relationship management processes and practices will involve all personnel in the organisation from leadership team to team member. Changes such as those described here will probably be associated with resistance through fear associated with uncertainty. The uncertainty could be about fears of:

- job loss;

- loss of organisational power;

- role de-skilling and consequent loss of income;

- increase in work load without appropriate compensation;

- unwanted additional responsibilities;

- requirements to acquire new skills;

- assignment of job roles that are not within their competencies.

Effective and credible communication to all affected stakeholders is the only cure for uncertainty.

A recognised change programme

Implementing stakeholder relationship management that introduces new processes and practices is change. Features of successful change programmes are:

- funding and resources are guaranteed;

- organisational (and management) agreement for the objectives (success criteria) of the change are clearly articulated at the beginning;

- a plan with milestones and deliverables is developed and maintained;

- stakeholders of the change are engaged (perhaps using the methodology that is being implemented);

- communication is frequent and regular to meet the needs of the programme and the stakeholders;

- the effectiveness of the communication is monitored (*step 4 engage; step 5: monitor*);

- progress is reviewed and communicated;

- successes are celebrated;

- *lessons learned* are reviewed at the end of the programme and learnings added to the knowledge assets of the organisation.

Research shows that change will not be successfully implemented through an announcement or a meeting or a training course. To be successful, managers must recognise:

- their role is ongoing, active and visible in all phases of the change;

- change management must be tailored to the organisation and the readiness of the organisation to accept this change;

- successful change requires an organisational and an individual approach.

Implementation of any change requires careful preparation. All people involved must be aware of the reasons for the change and how it will affect both individuals and their managers. They must also be willing to accept the change and its consequences.

Three essential steps for implementing change

These guidelines will be organised around three major aspects of any successful change management programme.[15] They are discussed briefly here to assist organisations in managing their change:

- Prepare for the change:

  - develop change management strategy;

  - organise the team (and their work);

  - develop the sponsor model.

---

15 These guidelines are based on the ADKAR methodology.

- Manage the change:

    - create the change management plans;

    - implement the plans;

    - develop competency in the organisation for dealing with change.

- Reinforce the change:

    - collect and analyse feedback;

    - diagnose gaps and manage resistance;

    - implement corrective action;

    - celebrate successes.

Communication to stakeholders (of the change) needs to be focused on frequent and planned messages containing answers to five important questions (Hiatt 2006):

1. Why change? How is this relevant to me?

2. What, exactly, do I need to do that's different?

3. How will I be measured and what are the consequences?

4. What tools and support do I get?

5. What's in it for me? WIIFM? For us?

All communication about the change programme should always seek to address some or all of these questions every time.

Measuring success

As with any change programme or organisational activity monitoring and measuring progress towards, or the achievement of, change, it is essential to have agreed success criteria. Some measures of successful change include:

- speed of adoption:

  - how well the change programme stays on schedule;

  - how quickly the change is adopted into normal organisational practice.

- utilisation rate:

  - overall level of participation in the programme;

  - overall level of tools and processes adopted.

- proficiency:

  - how staff perform with the new processes and tools;

  - are they achieving the expected performance?

- measurement by openly communicated criteria.

Conclusion

This chapter focused on what an organisation must do to continuously improve its stakeholder relationship management processes and practices. Descriptions of the 5 levels of SRMM are provided with details that should further assist an organisation in knowing its current level of maturity, what is involved with attaining the next *level*, and the ability to recognise when it has actually achieved that next *level*.

Changes such as those described are not trivial; they require commitment from all personnel involved in the change, but also encouragement and support from management. Other personnel in the organisation who may be affected by the change need to understand the reasons for the change, how they will be affected, and what they can expect to gain from it. This is all about communication: targeted communication and monitoring and measuring the effectiveness of that communication. Therefore the tools, techniques, processes and practices that have been described in Chapters 3 to 6 should be adopted to support this change.

Table 9.1   Guidelines for implementing SRMM

SRMM Level	Features	Methodology Steps	Reporting/ Tools	Comments
1. Ad hoc: some use of processes	Individuals recognise the need for stakeholder relationship management; may or may not use an existing methodology.	Generally focuses on simplified selected steps: *step 4: engage* and *step 5: monitor*.	Self-developed tools; Word templates; Spreadsheet lists.	Requires continuous and significant management 'push' to maintain impetus.
2. Procedural: focus on processes and tools	SHM introduced as part of the implementation of consistent processes (perhaps result of CMMI assessment).	Sometimes all five steps but truncated and simplified.	Standardised tools; Word templates; Spreadsheets with macros; Simple database.	Requires continuous and significant management 'push' to maintain impetus.
3. Relational: focus on the stakeholders and mutual benefits	Recognition of usefulness for competitor analysis, or support for mergers/ acquisition.	All five steps implemented. Move towards valuing insights /information in decision-making.	Fully functional tools; Spreadsheets with macros; Sophisticated databases.	Useful for specific applications or events; rarely with an intention of continuous application.
4. Integrated: methodology is repeatable and integrated	'Business as usual' application using the full methodology for all projects and selected operational work.	*Steps 1–5* with *step 4: engage* and *step 5: monitor* being vital for evidence of success.	Graphic reports, visualisation, engagement profiles, etc, used in management reports and KPIs.	The methodology and tools are used as a demonstration of repeatable application within that part of the organisation.
5. Predictive: used for health checks, predictive risk assessment, management:	Implementation of the full methodology and supporting tools.	*Steps 1–5.* 'Lessons Learned' & comparative data. Integrated data across programmes, etc.	Trend reporting, pro-active risk identification (unusual profiles). Comparison between projects and different categories of work.	Organisation-wide and complete focus on continuous improvement as competitive advantage.

Table 9.3   Characteristics of level 1

	Level 1 characteristics
Culture	
Experience	Individuals will apply stakeholder relationship management in the way that 'works for them' or has worked in other organisations.
Process	
Application	

Table 9.5   Characteristics of level 2

	Level 2 characteristics
Culture	An increased level of awareness of the importance of stakeholder relationship management; the awareness programmes that are part of the change programme from level 1 are raising awareness and willingness to participate.
Experience	Those involved in the activities using the structure of *step 4* and *step 5* have recognised the utility of the structured approach and the output for reporting and have taken this knowledge, awareness and willingness to other activities they are working on. While the majority of individuals in the organisation will apply stakeholder relationship management processes and practices in the way that 'works for them', an increasing number of personnel who have experienced the benefits of the practices introduced at the first level will be encouraged to use the practices in new assignments or new activities.
Process	
Application	

Table 9.7   Characteristics of level 3

	Level 3 characteristics
Culture	There are usually specific triggers for the change to a relational approach and a clear connection between an event or situation that will affect personnel in the organisation and actions implemented to avert or exploit the event or its consequences. Personnel, who may have previously resisted any change because they could not see any benefit for themselves, will be more motivated to support the change.
Experience	Personnel who had previously been involved with using stakeholder relationship management processes and practices at level 2 or even level 1 will be familiar with the tools already in use. A central support unit is often introduced at this stage, enabling the organisation to improve its stakeholder relationship management through the support of this unit and possible outside expertise.

Table 9.7   *Concluded*

Process	The full spectrum of stakeholder relationship management processes and practices will be used, with management support also being given in the form of funding and resourcing for support and training from the central support unit.
Application	Within the boundaries of the events or situations that have triggered this improvement, there will be consensus about the usefulness of the stakeholder relationship management processes and practices to achieve the goals of that particular area and perhaps even the leadership team.

Table 9.9   **Characteristics of level 4**

	Level 4 characteristics
Culture	Management expectation that all activities apply stakeholder relationship management means that the ***Stakeholder*** Circle methodology (or any other similar methodology) will most likely be applied to stakeholder relationship management in the organisation. However, while the information will be gathered about stakeholders as part of the practice of stakeholder relationship management, the application of this information to successful techniques for communication does not necessarily follow. The thrust of any awareness or change management programme in relation to level 4 must include training on communication techniques and encouragement for advanced communication.[*]
Experience	There should be personnel in the organisation who have experienced the benefits of successful stakeholder relationship management. They should also have developed the competencies and the willingness to operate within the power structures of the organisation for more effective stakeholder relationship management. This experience must be exploited for the benefit of the organisation. Those who have attained this level of competence should be encouraged to mentor others.
Process	
Application	Considered to be part of the regular toolkit to be used on all organisational activities.

* Chapter 5.

Table 9.11   Characteristics of level 5

	Level 5 characteristics
Culture	The culture of stakeholder relationship management will be included in the thinking and daily work of the organisation. The central support unit will provide the appropriate level of training and support to ensure its continuation.
Experience	Regular training and coaching reinforces the culture of continuous improvement. Inexperienced team members will have access to more experienced colleagues for assistance and guidance in stakeholder communication and other stakeholder relationship management tools and techniques.
Process	The full set of *steps* of the **Stakeholder** *Circle* methodology have been standardised, compliance is measured and continuous improvement of the process is supported by the central support unit and management.
Application	The use of the **Stakeholder** *Circle* methodology is considered to be the best support for stakeholder relationship management within that department.

10

Conclusion

My reason for writing this book was to consolidate in one place a practical set of guidelines and information about managing stakeholder relationships for three different groups:

1. Students and researchers: I want to stimulate you with ideas about stakeholder theory, both recent and historical, and the importance of stakeholder relationship management to organisational success in order to encourage more research into this fascinating area. In particular I hope to stimulate interest in researching the concept of stakeholder relationship management maturity more widely.

2. Practitioners: I want to provide the individuals and groups within organisations who struggle daily with relationship management and communication, with a practical resource to make your job easier.

3. Executives: by providing a more strategic, measurable, flexible approach to implementing a stakeholder relationship management methodology I hope to make it an easy decision to invest more funds, resource and commitment into improving relationship management in your organisations.

The book has three sections. Each of them can be useful on its own, or the three together can be used as a handbook for organisations seeking to improve their reputation and their bottom line through better management of relationships both within and outside of its boundaries. The three sections are:

1. Framework;

2. Guidebook;

3. Implementation.

Section I: Framework

Section I provided an overview of the importance of stakeholders to an organisation's reputation and bottom line, using the disruptions of the opening of British Airways' Heathrow Terminal 5 early in 2008 as an example. Discussions of the emerging understanding of the importance of stakeholders, and an examination of a wider concept of 'who can be a stakeholder' leads to the view that the success or failure of any activity is usually determined by the stakeholder's perception of success or failure. The theme of Section I is that it is essential to know who belongs to the stakeholder community for each and every activity and communicate effectively to manage their expectations, and therefore their perceptions, if you want your activity to be seen as a success.

Section II: Guidebook

Section II is a *'how-to'* guide. With detailed descriptions of each of the five *steps* of the **Stakeholder** Circle methodology, everything an organisation needs to know to *identify, prioritise, visualise, engage* and *monitor* their stakeholder relationships is defined.

Section III: Implementation

Section III introduces for the first time the Stakeholder Relationship Management Maturity (SRMM) model. SRMM is a five-level model that provides an organisation with the ability to recognise its current level of readiness to implement stakeholder relationship management processes and practices. Once the organisation understands its current level it can use the guidelines included in the model to plan a programme to achieve the next level of stakeholder relationship management. The descriptions of each level also provide the organisation with a means to monitor the implementation programme to know when it has achieved its objectives.

Origin of the Know-How Supporting the Methodology and Guidelines

The tacit knowledge supporting the methodologies and guidelines in this book are the result of:

- my own experiences as a:

  - project and programme manager in corporations;

  - senior manager – sponsor, business owner.

- research and publication of the dissertation for my Doctor of Project Management (DPM) at RMIT;[1]

- commercial development of the *Stakeholder* Circle tool (SIMS) and its implementation in organisations;

- feedback from seminars, workshops and consultancy in many areas of the world;

- discussions with colleagues, both face-to-face and electronically.

The results are, I hope, a practical synthesis of ideas and practices that can be usefully applied to any organisation. The journey is not over. This book is only a staging point. Research innovation and the changing business culture worldwide will continue to push the frontiers of knowledge and practice in this fascinating area of stakeholder engagement and management.

Communicate! Communicate! Communicate!

One of the recurring themes of this book and indeed of stakeholder relationships in general is the need to communicate, communicate and communicate again. As discussed in Chapter 2, communication is the only tool available to build and maintain relationships between stakeholders and the activity. The progress reports, risk and issue action plans and financial reports as well as meetings, emails, formal letters and face-to-face discussions are all communication, and they all influence perception. They should be crafted and used wisely.

The whole purpose of understanding who matters, who is key, and who is important at any particular time is to understand who needs information and the form that information must take. The stakeholder mapping processes described in Chapter 4 are all attempts to understand and reveal the members of the stakeholder community, their expectations and attitudes *in preparation for communication*. This

---

1   www.rmit.edu

book provides guidelines on how a single activity or a whole organisation can identify and prioritise stakeholders and then develop targeted communication. Communication is the subject of a whole book in itself (and there are many good ones). Chapter 6 has an overview of essential aspects of communication in general, and Chapter 9 describes important elements of communication for change programmes, but they are not intended to replace more in-depth resources focused on effective communication. The *Stakeholder Circle* is focused on determining *who* to communicate with at any particular time and not *how* to communicate.

Relationships are two-sided connections, where both parties have expectations that need to be understood and managed. Because relationships are about people or groups of people the connections are never static. The relationships within or between organisations and their activities are no different. It is not sufficient to do the stakeholder analysis, develop a map and implement a communication plan only once. As people's lives change their views of situations will also change: agreements for support, cooperation or supply that has been given sincerely at one time may not be honoured at a later time. In the same way, disagreements and confrontation may be modified or neutralised with the passage of time or change of circumstances, or even as a result of well-managed communication and relationship management. It is therefore essential to continually review the stakeholder community and modify approaches where necessary. The methodology described in this book provides the means to do so with its:

- structured but flexible approach;

- standard rating system that supports trend reporting;

- diverse mapping options, from the simple MS Word document that can be manually completed to the sophisticated SIMS database that can provide multi-dimensional information about the current stakeholder community; and at the same time storing the history of previous relationships to enable the organisation to measure the success of its efforts or have evidence that it needs to try other approaches.

This book has been designed for flexibility. It should support organisations to manage change of any type whether it is:

- projects or programmes;

- business change or business process re-engineering (BPR);

- mergers and acquisitions (M&A) or competitor analysis;

- corporate social responsibility (CSR) or culture changes;

- implementing large constructions (such as Heathrow T5 or the Sydney Opera House) or delivering a small internal software upgrade.

I wish you well in your endeavours and hope that these ideas can help organisations and the people within them to be more successful.

References

AccountAbility, (2006). *Stakeholder Engagement Standard* (AA1000SES), London, Institute of Social and Ethical Accountability.

Bourne, L. and D.H.T. Walker, (2003). *Tapping into the Power Lines – A 3rd Dimension of Project Management Beyond Leading and Managing,* Proceedings of 17th World Congress on Project Management, Moscow, Russia.

Briner, W., C. Hastings, M. Geddes, (1996). *Project Leadership,* Aldershot, Hampshire, UK, Gower.

Carnegie Mellon Institute, (2006). 'The Capability Maturity Model: CMMI for Development', *The SEI Series in Software Engineering,* Reading, Massachusetts, Addison-Wesley.

Collins, J. and J. Porras, (1995). *Built to Last. Successful Habits of Visionary Companies,* London, Century, Random House.

Csikszentmihalyi, M. (1997). *Creativity: Flow and the Psychology of Discovery and Invention,* New York, HarperCollins.

Done, K. (2008). 'Airport regulator slates BAA ownership', *Financial Times,* London.

Fletcher, A., J. Guthrie, P. Steane, G. Roos, S. Pike, (2003). 'Mapping Stakeholder Perceptions for a Third Sector Organisation', *Journal of Intellectual Capital* 4(4): 505–527.

Freeman, R.E. (1984). *Strategic Management: A Stakeholder Approach,* Boston MA, Pitman Publishing.

French, W., A and J. Granrose, (1995). *Practical Business Ethics,* New Jersey, Prentice Hall.

Frooman, J. (1999). 'Stakeholders Influence Strategies', *Academy of Management Review,* 24(2): 191–205.

Glasser, W. (1998). *The Quality School: Managing Students Without Coercion,* New York, Harper Collins.

Granovetter, M.S. (1973). 'The Strength of Weak Ties', *American Journal of Sociology,* 78(6): 1360–1380.

Hiatt, J.M. (2006). *ADKAR: A Model for Change in Business, Government and our Community*, Loveland, Colorado, USA, Prosci Research.

Hillson, D.A. (1997). 'Towards a Risk Maturity Model', *International Journal of Project and Business Risk Management* 1(1): 35–45.

Hillson, D.A. and R. Murray-Webster, (2005). *Understanding and Managing Risk Attitude*, Aldershot, UK, Gower.

House of Commons Transport Committee (2008). *The Opening of Heathrow Terminal 5*, London, The Stationery Office Limited.

KPMG, (2005). 'Global IT Project Management Survey: How Committed are You?' Sydney, Australia, KPMG Information Risk Management Practice.

Lemon, W. F., J. Bowitz, J. Burn, and R. Hackney, (2002). 'Information Systems Project Failure: A Comparative Study of Two Countries', *Journal of Global Information Management*, April-June 2002: 28–28.

Lovell, R. J. (1993). 'Power and the Project Manager', *International Journal of Project Management*, 11(2): 73–78.

McGrath, J.E. (1984). *Groups: Interaction and Performance*, New Jersey, Prentice Hall.

Mitchell, R.K., B.R. Agle, D. Wood, (1997). 'Toward a Theory of Stakeholder Identification and Salience: Defining the Principle of Who and What really Counts', *Academy of Management Review*, 22(4): 853–888.

Murray, P. (2004). *The saga of the Sydney Opera House: The Dramatic Story of the Design and Construction of the Icon of Modern Australia*, London UK, Spon Press.

Murray-Webster, R. and D.A. Hillson, (2008). *Managing Group Risk Attitude*, Aldershot, UK, Gower.

Murray-Webster, R. and P. Simon, (2008). 'Make Sense of Stakeholder Mapping with Sensible Stakeholder Mapping: Lucid Thought #24', *Lucid Thought*, Lucidus Consulting.

Pinto, J. K. (1998). *Power and Politics in Project Management*, Pennsylvania, Project Management Institute.

Playfair, W. (1801). *Commercial and Political Atlas*, London, J.Wallis.

Potts, K. (2006). *Project Management and the Changing Nature of the Quantity Surveying Profession – Heathrow Terminal 5 Case Study*, COBRA 2006, London, The RICS, London.

Project Management Institute, (2008). *A Guide to the Project Management Body of Knowledge (PMBOK)*, Pennsylvania, USA, Project Management Institute, Inc.

Project Management Institute, (2008). *Organizational Project Management Maturity Model (OPM3)*, Pennsylvania, USA, Project Management Institute Inc.

Rock, D. (2006). *Quiet Leadership: Six Steps to Transforming Performance at Work*, New York, HarperCollins.

Rowley, T.J. (1997). 'Moving Beyond Dyadic Ties: A Network Theory of Stakeholder Influences', *Academy of Management Review*, 22(4): 887–910.

Sauer, C. (1993). *Why Information Systems Fail: A Case Study Approach*, Henley-on-Thames, Alfred Waller.

Savage, G.T., T.W. Nix, C. Whitehead and J. Blair, (1991). 'Strategies for Assessing and Managing Organisational Stakeholders', *Academy of Management Executive*, 5(2): 61–75.

Software Engineering Institute, S. (2006). 'CMMI Overview', from http://www.sei.cmu.edu/cmmi/adoption/: retrieved Jan 13, 2009.

Stacey, R.D. (2001). *Complex Responsive Processes in Organisations; Learning and Knowledge Creation*, London, Routledge.

Stoney, C. and D. Winstanley (2001). 'Stakeholding: Confusion or Utopia? Mapping the Conceptual Terrain', *Journal of Management Studies*, 38(5): 603–626.

Sweet, R. (2008). 'The T5 Effect', *International Construction Review*, (Quarter 2, 2008): 10–14.

Tague, N.R. (2004). *The Quality Toolbox*, ASQ Quality Press.

Tufte, E. (2006). *Beautiful Evidence*, Cheshire, Connecticut, Graphics Press.

Wainer, H. and I. Spence (2005). *Playfair's Commercial and Political Atlas and Statistical Breviary: Introduction to Reprint edition*. New York, Cambridge University Press.

Walker, D.H.T., L. Bourne, and A. Shelley, (2008). 'Influence, Stakeholder Mapping and Visualisation', *Construction, Management and Economics* (26): 645–658.

Walker, D.H.T., L. Bourne, et al., (2008). 'Stakeholders and the Supply Chain', *Procurement Systems: A Cross-Industry Project Management Perspective*, D.H.T. Walker and S. Rowlinson (eds), London, Taylor and Francis.

Youker, R. (1992). 'Managing the International Project Environment', *International Journal of Project Management* 10(4): 219–226.

Index

About the Author

Lynda Bourne DPM, PMP, FAIM, CMACS is an award-winning project manager, management consultant and trainer with 25 years' professional industry experience. She is the CEO and founder of Stakeholder Management Pty Ltd.

Lynda was the Project Management Institute (PMI) Australia's *Project Manager of the Year* for 2003. She has also been included in PMI's inaugural list of *25 Influential Women in Project Management* (2006) and is included in the 2007, 2008 and 2009 editions of *Who's Who of Australian Women*. Lynda received support in the form of tuition scholarships from both PMI and the Australian Institute of Project Management (AIPM) during the 2004/2005 academic year for work associated with completing her Doctor of Project Management (DPM) thesis. For her thesis, Lynda investigated the dynamics of the interaction between project teams and their key stakeholders.

A recognised international speaker and author on the topic of stakeholder relationship management and the **Stakeholder** *Circle*® methodology, she has presented at conferences and seminars in Europe, Russia, Asia, New Zealand, Australia and the US to audiences from the IT, construction, defence and mining industries.

Lynda has extensive experience in the senior ranks of corporations and as a senior Programme Manager specialising in delivery of IT and other business-related projects. Lynda's career has combined practical project experience with business management roles and academic research to deliver successful projects that meet stakeholders' expectations.

CD Contents

Software

SIMS DATABASE

30-day trial version of Stakeholder Information Management System (SIMS), the database version of software support for the **Stakeholder** *Circle*® methodology, as described in Chapter 4 (see Figures 4.9 and 4.10 for examples of its use). Any data entered will be saved for importing to a commercial version of the tool.

SOAP TEMPLATES

Word template: *stakeholder-on-a-page* (SOAP), as described in Chapters 4 and 9 (see Figures 4.11 and 9.2); Word 2003 and 2007 versions.

Resources

QUICK REFERENCE GUIDE

PDF 'Quick Reference Guide' to help apply the **Stakeholder** *Circle*® methodology.

SELF-RUNNING POWERPOINT DEMOS

A short and a longer version – overviewing the **Stakeholder** *Circle*® methodology.

White Papers

P038: The Paradox of Project Control.

P047: Visualising Stakeholder Influence, Two Australian Examples.

P062: Influence, Stakeholder Mapping and Visualisation.

P074: Developing Stakeholder Engagement Maturity in APM Terminals Management BV: An International Case Study.

P077: From Commander to Sponsor: Managing Upwards in a Project Environment.

P085: Practice Note: Advancing Theory and Practice for Advancing Stakeholder Management in Organisations.

P087: Introducing a Stakeholder Management Methodology into the EU.

If you have found this book useful you may be interested in other titles from Gower

Making the Business Case:
Proposals that Succeed for Projects that Work
Ian Gambles
Paperback: 978-0-566-08745-5

Training for Project Management: Volumes 1 to 3
Ian Stokes
A4 Looseleaf: 978-0-566-08869-8; 978-0-566-08870-4; 978-0-566-08871-1

Managing Project Uncertainty
David Cleden
Paperback: 978-0-566-08840-7

Project Governance
Ralf Müller
Paperback: 978-0-566-08866-7

Practical Schedule Risk Analysis
David Hulett
Hardback: 978-0-566-08790-5

Images of Projects
Mark Winter and Tony Szczepanek
Hardback: 978-0-566-08716-5

Managing Risk in Projects
David Hillson
Paperback: 978-0-566-08867-4

Strategic Project Risk Appraisal and Management
Elaine Harris
Paperback: 978-0-566-08848-3

GOWER